DELUSIONS OF

GRANDEUR

How To Become More Than You Ever

Dreamed Possible

To Jo,
Wishing you the Very Best
for the future,
Love
Mark xx

MARK LLEWHELLIN

DEDICATION

This book is dedicated to the love of my life, my little miracle, Léon James Llewhellin, who I love more than anyone in the world. You are kind, thoughtful, well balanced and you are already achieving great things in your life!

Words cannot describe how much I love you and how proud I am of the person you are.

This book is also dedicated to you the reader. May you also have delusions of grandeur and live your dreams!

Table of Contents

INTRODUCTION

Delusion definition:

1. A false belief or opinion about yourself or your situation.
2. The act of believing or making yourself believe something that is not true.

- Oxford Dictionary

Grandeur definition:

1. The quality of being great and impressive in appearance.

- Oxford Dictionary

Delusions of grandeur definition:

The belief that you are more important or powerful than you really are.

- Cambridge Dictionary

Okay, so here we go with the first question, why another personal development book?

The reality is, there can never only be one book on personal development that is relevant to everyone as we all interpret things differently.

We all like different stories, we all have different needs, we are all unique and there aren't just one or two stories to tell - there are hundreds if not thousands, of inspiring stories to tell.

It's the same with any genre, whether it's romance, thriller, or action and adventure. How many times have we seen an underdog go out in a movie against impossible odds, win the battle and get the girl (or guy) and become a big success?

It's a common story, but it's a story that we all love, and each story is told differently.

Writing about personal development is also what I love to write about because I've seen the changes books like this have made in peoples lives as well as my own.

It seems like a bold subtitle, "How To Become The Person You Dream Of Becoming," but I can confidently put that subtitle because I am now the person I always dreamed of being. And I know that if I can become the person I dreamed of becoming, achieve the things I once dreamed about and live a life that was once an impossibility for me, then anyone else can do the same.

All I've done is put together the research to get the very best information out there from people who have achieved brilliant things in their lives.

2

Yes, there are things that you and I can learn from our own experiences, but much of what we learn is from other people.

I'm hoping that this book will give you a shortcut to achieving your own goals so you can avoid many of the mistakes that I made.

So how did this book come about?

A few years ago, a friend messaged me and said she was upset because someone had messaged her and said a few unkind things about me.

The person that messaged my friend was one of my old school friends.

As often happens in life, you leave school and you drift away from many of your friends, at least that was the case before the days of Facebook, and it was certainly the case with me and him.

Now after over 20 years of almost no contact with him, he turns up out of the blue and decides he isn't happy with what I'm doing with my life.

He could see that I have big dreams and goals but instead of saying things like, "go for it," or "I hope Mark makes it happen," or "I sincerely wish Mark all the luck in the world," he thought it would be better to message my friend (who he didn't even know) and tell her that I have delusions of grandeur.

My friend who told me about this situation was terribly upset about this guy's actions and couldn't work out why someone was ripping into me like this.

3

Not only this, I noticed every now and again he was posting on my Facebook comments section things that weren't exactly what you would call supportive.

It's one of those situations where someone is trying to publicly tear you down, but they say they're only joking when you ask them about it.

So, what was it that made him turn up out of the blue, slag me off on my Facebook comments section and message my friend telling her that I'd lost the plot and I had delusions of grandeur?

Who knows?

People have their own reasons for doing things; in the end I just deleted his ass off my Facebook!

If someone's either stabbing you in your back or constantly trying to belittle you then you need to get him or her out of your life!

It's not so easy with family members but at the very least, you'll need to limit the amount of time you're around that person.

This might sound a bit harsh to some people, but you need positive encouraging people around you if you want to achieve your goals and even more importantly if you want a healthy state of mind!

I love the film 'Limitless' because it explores the potential of the human mind and the possibilities for people if they open their mind, gain knowledge, and take action.

Bradley Cooper's character – 'Eddie Morra' is having a tremendous amount of success in a short space of time.

Ok, he's taken some sort of magic pill that opens up his mind so he can use his brain better than he's ever done before.

I can't promise that this book will be like the pill Bradley's character used in the film, but I can promise that if you have an open mind, this book can give you a push in the right direction to achieve some of your dreams and help you become the person you dream of being.

Because of Morra's success, he soon gets a meeting with Robert De Niro's character - 'Carl Van Loon,' who is a super wealthy investor. Van Loon asks Cooper, "What's your secret?"

Morra explains that his success was down to research, massive research and how mass psychology works.

Morra explains that he does have a formula for success and one of Van Loon's advisors cuts in and says that Morra has delusions of grandeur.

Morra says, "I don't have delusions of grandeur, I have an actual recipe for grandeur!"

This book will also provide a recipe for you getting what you want in life.

It's not the normal recipe book like Jamie Oliver produces and I probably won't say 'fuck' anywhere near as much as what Gordon Ramsay does.

Have I got all the answers?

No, but what I will give you in this book is some of the recipes I've used to become the person I once dreamed of becoming.

I once saw a clip on YouTube where Will Smith was talking passionately about 'not' being realistic.

He's right!

Everyone who has ever created or invented something awesome was a dreamer, had unrealistic expectations and was thought of by some, as having delusions of grandeur!

Now to contradict that slightly, I interviewed athletics world record holder Colin Jackson about achieving goals and his advice was to be realistic!

When I questioned him about this he said that when he started off in his athletics career, it wasn't realistic to assume he would break a world record in his early years.

So, who was right?

Was it Colin Jackson or was it Will Smith?

Well, they've both achieved international success at an extremely high level, and the fact is that both of them are right!

In other words, there is more than one way to achieve your goals; some people have different thought processes, some people have different techniques, but there are certain things that they all do that lead to success and I will explore some of these things in this book.

I'm not naturally brilliant at things and there are many things I can still learn and have much to improve on.

However, where I am now compared to where I was, is quite frankly…a fucking miracle!

WHO GETS DELUSIONS OF GRANDEUR?

"I have a dream."
- *Martin Luther King, Jr.*

So, who gets 'delusions of grandeur?'

According to certain psychiatrists and psychologists it's people who are crazy.

Yes, there are people that are locked up in a mental facility who think they are a celebrity, a member of high society, the President, an army general or an important member of their community.

However, after many years of studying people who have achieved great things, I can confidently say almost all of the successful people I have interviewed or read about, all first thought they were more than their current circumstances showed.

They are:

- People, who were massively overweight but went on to build an awesome physique for themselves.
- People who had no money but went on to make big money.
- People who were useless academically in school but went on to build successful companies.

- People who didn't get any attention from the opposite or same sex early on in life but turned that around later in life.
- People who were overlooked by the teachers in school and later went on to teach others through public speaking and developed into great leaders.
- People who had little self-confidence but became super confident.
- People who were not gifted at athletics or sports but went on to achieve great things in those fields.
- People who thought they wouldn't be someone special, but they became the type of person that they once dreamed about becoming.

If you're anything like me and the people I've interviewed, you'll also have so called delusions of grandeur, crazy ideas, dreams and goals - but having these things are only half of what you need.

The next thing you will need to do to achieve your dreams is to take action!

Not random haphazard action, but precise, massive, kick-ass action!

You are already taking action by reading this book and even though you may feel good at the end of reading it, I sincerely hope that you take action towards your own dreams and goals.

Some people turn into professional students just by reading books or attending courses but sadly never take that next step to make their dreams come true.

Don't be one of those people!

IS EVERYTHING POSSIBLE?

"To be or not to be, that is the question."

-   *William Shakespeare (from Hamlet)*

Take a look back at your life and think about how things you once thought were impossible are now a reality!

Take a look at the technology that is around us today and take a look at the things you have achieved in your own life.

Many things that were impossible at first, are now not just possible but commonplace.

However, I'm not one of those people that think that if you believe you can achieve something, it will automatically become a reality, 100%, no questions asked.

The reason for this is because there are thousands, if not millions, of people who believed that 'one-day' their dream would come true, and for one reason or another it didn't.

We may not be able to make all our dreams come true, but what I do know is that if you believe something is possible, you've got a much better chance of making it a reality!

I'm also not an advocate of the phrase 'anything is possible,' somethings just aren't.

Example:

Swimming around in boiling water naked for a few hours and living to tell the tale.

Okay, somebody might develop a special swimming suit in years to come where you can swim around in boiling water, but I did say naked.

Maybe in a hundred or a thousand years from now someone will develop some sort of serum where your body becomes immune to the conditions around us, like some kind of Superman/Wolverine person.

As crazy as that may sound, there are already creatures on this planet that can live in extremely hot and very cold places.

One example of something that can withstand extreme temperatures is the Wood Frog.

Wood frogs are badass when it comes to surviving the cold for a long time. Scientists at the University of Alaska Fairbanks discovered that wood frogs use a substance called a cryoprotectant that is made up of antifreeze compounds and proteins which enable them to survive for over six months being chilled at an average temperature of -14.6°C (6°F) and could go as low as -18°C (0°F).

However, when it comes to the toughest, hardest, and most badass all round critters on the planet, the Water Bear (otherwise known as Tardigrade) is the King, the Daddy, the

Don and Numero Uno of surviving so-called impossible elements!

This microscopic creature can survive temperatures as low as -273°C (459°F) and heat over 150°C (302°F) and you can currently find them on vacation in the depths of the ocean, Himalayan mountain tops, tropical rainforests, the Antarctic and mud volcanoes.

They can withstand pressures over 5 times more than the pressure from the deepest ocean trenches.

They can survive radiation doses hundreds of times higher than the lethal dose for humans and can pop in and out of space for short breaks.

If they are in a place where there's no food or water - not a problem as they can survive for over 3 years without either.

Scientists from Oxford and Harvard universities looked at probabilities of Doomsday events such as a meteorite hitting the Earth, a supernova blast, and a gamma-ray burst.

They concluded that the Water Bear would probably survive such doomsday events.

At the time of writing, COVID–19 is sweeping through the planet and sadly taking many peoples' lives.

Spanish flu (also known as the 1918 flu pandemic) had an estimated death toll of up to 50 million people.

In-between 1347 to 1351, the most devastating plague in recorded history hit the world.

The Black Death, otherwise known as the 'Great Bubonic Plague' resulted in the deaths of an estimated 75 to 200 million people. However, not even the Black Death could wipe out the Water Bear. Astrophysicist Rafael Alves Batista told Casey Smith of National Geographic that the Water Bear species has existed for at least 520 million years and survived multiple mass extinctions!

Now that's one resilient little fucker, and I thought that grizzly bears were tough as nails!

While all of this sounds very science fiction like, it's only a matter of time before scientists and inventors produce more and more things that were once thought of as impossible.

As we've gone from the horse and cart to the space rocket all within 150 years, it's getting harder and harder to say what is possible and what isn't.

Although it might sound a bit Jurassic Parky where they extract the DNA out of a preserved mosquito that's got a bit of dinosaur in it, and with a few scientists and a lab, they produce a dinosaur; who's to say that in a thousand or a million years from now (if the human race survives that long) this can't happen?

Maybe they'll be able to extract DNA from a water bear, cross it with a flea (that can jump 200 times their body length), cross it with a greater wax moth (who's hearing is 150 times better than ours and add a spider that can walk on walls.

For a bit of longevity throw in the atoms from the Methuselah (a pine tree said to be almost 5,000 years old) or perhaps even better, the Turritopsis dohrnii AKA the immortal jellyfish which transforms its cells into new types of cells and then goes back to an immature state!

In theory, growing old and young again; making the jellyfish biologically immortal.

Then you have what would be considered the ultimate thing to have...immortality.

Whether it's from the 1986 movie 'Highlander,' where immortals walk this earth looking to chop off each other's heads with swords that weigh about the same as a small buffalo. Or whether it's the 1989 'Indiana Jones And The Last Crusade' movie, where Indie (played by Harrison Ford) is looking for The Holy Grail that you can drink from and gain immortality; immortality is right up there on many peoples Ultimate Wish List!

Just as the writers of 'Star Trek' envisaged things before they became a reality, scientists, inventors and other creative people are constantly making the impossible possible.

The question for us though, is what will become of our lives?

Will we achieve things that we can be proud of, or will we look back at our lives and be disappointed?

"To be or not to be," is something that we have more control over than what we may first think!

Everything that is man-made has come from someone's grand idea and the longer you live, the more you can appreciate what has changed and what advances the human race has made.

At the time of writing, I'm only 46 years old.

To children my son's age, I'm pretty old, but to some people, I'm just a young pup.

Either way, I've seen some amazing things happen over my lifetime.

The invention of the mobile phone, the MRI machine, the GPS, the laser beam, no not the one that kills people in James Bond movies, what use is that?! I'm talking about the laser beam that whitens teeth. What would our celebrities do without it?

In 1978, genetic engineering created the first synthetic 'human' insulin.

In 1998, we got the MP3 player and thank the heavens for the Zenith Radio Corporation and Eugene Polly who invented the TV remote control in the 1950's.

Even in my cars, I've seen the changes over the years.

I got my first car when I was 18 because I'd had enough of driving from Wales to Scotland and half-freezing to death on my motorbike.

My first car was an old Ford Escort.

Yes it was a piece of shit that had wind up windows and a small basic engine, but I didn't care - it was something that I never had before, so I enjoyed driving it towards Scotland until the police pulled me over and confiscated it.

Apparently you need a driving licence, insurance, M.O.T and car tax to drive up the motorway. Ahhhhh, the things you do when you're young!

As the years go by, you get these Gucci little things that we take for granted today like central locking, ABS brakes, electric windows, air-conditioning, and electric seats. In my latest car (a Jaguar XF), it doesn't even have a key (not too uncommon these days); you simply unlock the car with a key fob.

You get in and you push a start button that flashes like a snazzy red heartbeat. When you press that, the engine starts and a little round metal thingie (that's my technical name for it) for the gearbox pops up out of the centre console like something you'd see inside Dr Who's Tardis.

It also has flappy paddles on the steering wheel, so I can change gear if I want to drive it manually...amazing!

Think of your own first car, what was it like?

Even if you are only 17 years old today, you'll still be aware of some of the changes that have happened in the automotive industry over the years.

When I visited the car museum in Coventry it had a car there that you had to windup to start it, on the other end of the scale it also had jet-powered cars.

All of these things that seem quite insignificant now were once a really big deal.

When you have a big dream many people will be quick to think or say, "you have to be realistic," but if everyone thought like that we would still be living in caves and saying the words "ug ug" to each other.

Every material thing commonly available now was once thought of as impossible and unrealistic.

As I write this I'm looking around in my bedroom and looking at one of the simplest things in it. I'm going to say wallpaper is something that is fairly simple (at least compared to the TV, laptop, iPad and Samsung smart phone).

Today wallpaper is no big deal, but it wasn't around in the 13th century and was thought of as unrealistic and impossible to make back then.

To make the vinyl base for wallpaper you need stabilising powder, a lot of plastic pellets, solvent, the beaters, and you have to do many other things to make wallpaper.

Imagine you're standing in a cave or a forest and someone asks you to make a plastic pellet.

The chances are you have no idea how to make plastic, which is the same as me because I didn't have a fucking Scooby Doo how to make plastic before I looked at it on YouTube.

Apparently you'll need coal, natural gas, minerals, plants and crude oil to make it. Can you see my point?

Making something like plastic at one point was totally impossible and unrealistic but that's the way it is with any new thing.

Whether it's something material you want or something physical you want to achieve, there are people who will say that your goal is unrealistic.

They will think that you have delusions of grandeur.

However, if you have the right mindset, what may seem impossible for some people can become your reality!

QUESTION EVERYTHING

"The important thing is not to stop questioning."

\-   *Albert Einstein*

If you believe that you're not destined for great things then you won't achieve great things but that's just because you told yourself you won't.

Don't get me wrong here, when I say achieve great things, I don't mean you have to be the next Nelson Mandela or Mother Teresa!

I'm talking about what you think is great and what you would love to achieve personally.

If somebody else thinks what you're trying to achieve is no big deal then that's fine but it's also totally irrelevant!

If you want to achieve something then believe in yourself and go after it!

Just because you believe something, whether you've made up this belief or someone's told you what to believe, it doesn't mean that he or she or you are right!

It's the same, as just because you hear about something or read it; it doesn't mean it's true.

Here are some examples of what I mean:

Many people believe that bulls get mad when they see the colour red.

It's a common belief that bulls charge when they see red, but is this true or false?

To be honest, I don't really care, but apparently when bulls aren't being grabbed by the horns or fucking up China shops, they charge at anything that is red!

However, when Sky One's MythBusters programme did experiments with red objects, which included a life-size cut-out of a red man, they found that the colour red didn't make the bull angry.

What did piss the bull off was movement!

So, it's movement that makes a bull charge and not the colour red.

The expression, "As blind as a bat" has been with me for as long as I can remember.

So, is it true that bats are blind?

Not according to most online resources including National Geographic, who asked Rob Mies (Executive Director for the Organisation for Bat Conservation) if bats are blind?

Mies said this wasn't true and the larger bats can see three times better than humans!

If you ask most people in the UK (and many other countries around the world) where was Jesus born, they will probably tell you he was born in Bethlehem in a barn or in a stable.

However, when I went to Bethlehem, I was taken to the place where Jesus was supposedly born.

I was thinking to myself, how the fuck is that barn still standing after 2000 years!

They must have used some kick ass wood preserver made by God himself!

So, my girlfriend and me jumped on a bus and ended up in a tiny cave (that later had a church built around it) where Jesus was said to have been born.

To make matters more confusing, Christiananswers.net says that the Bible does not mention a barn, a stable or a cave. It only mentions a manger!

So, what is the truth?

To be honest I don't know - I wasn't there.

Will it make a difference to your life where Jesus was born?

Probably not.

But it does give you food for thought and at the very least you can see that finding the truth isn't always as easy as you may first think.

So, what's the point of all this and how does it relate to you becoming more than you ever dreamed possible?

The point is, if you're anything like what I was, then you may not think that you're capable of becoming the person you want to be, and you may not think you will achieve the things you want to achieve.

Maybe someone tells you that you're having delusions of grandeur and you'll never achieve bigger things than you've already achieved.

Or maybe it's you that's always told yourself that you're not good enough?

Maybe once upon a time you were like me and you believed that bats are blind and bulls charge at red things, but all of a sudden you were presented with the hard facts and you changed your mind in an instant.

More importantly, you changed your belief in an instant and that is one of the goals in this book.

I know for a fact that you can become more than you have become, and there are still a lot of great things out there that you can achieve!

The placebo effect has been talked about and studied by many of the top medical professionals.

For those who don't know what a placebo is, it is usually a tablet or capsule, which contains no drug and is given to a patient to test whether the active drug works effectively.

According to www.nhs.uk, one well-known example of the placebo effect was done in 1996 where scientists got a group of people together and told them that they were going to take part in a new painkiller study.

The painkiller smelled like medicine, but it had no medicine in it, it was a fake!

Each student had the painkiller applied on one finger and the other finger had nothing applied to it.

Then each student had his or her finger squeezed in a vice.

The students said that they felt far less pain in the finger that had the so-called painkiller applied to it.

Their expectation and belief created real results even though the finger had no pain killing medicine on it!

The mind is an immensely powerful thing and your beliefs will create your reality!

The British National Health Service report went on to say: "placebos can get amazing results. The placebo is real and powerful!

The placebo effect points to the importance of perception and the brain's role in physical health."

The placebo is believed to reduce pain by changing people's perception and it releases the brains natural pain killer...endorphins.

Endorphins are released through exercise, laughing, sex and having quality relationships with friends and loved ones.

Having quality relationships with people comes down to how well you can get along with other people and getting on well with other people is something I plan to write about in a later book.

Endorphins have a similar chemical structure to Morphine - they lower stress levels, boost confidence, make you feel good and they give you a sense of peace and security.

When I was living with one of my ex girlfriends, I suggested that maybe she should try decaffeinated coffee rather than her normal caffeinated. She didn't seem too keen on the idea, but I convinced her just to try so she did.

I bought her the same coffee brand but just in its decaffeinated form. After trying the decaf, she told me that she didn't feel as awake and that it didn't taste as good, so I put her back on the caffeinated coffee... or at least that's what she thought.

While she was out one day I bought her the caffeinated coffee, but I did the ole switcheroo and tipped the caffeinated coffee into the decaf jar and I poured the decaf into the caffeinated jar.

Then one morning we were in the kitchen and I said to her, "I suppose you want your caffeinated coffee?"

While showing her the jar labelled as regular caffeinated coffee (that had the decaf in), she looked at me with a big smile, batted her cute little eyes at me and said, "yes please."

She seemed happy that she was drinking her 'so called' caffeinated coffee again and a few days later I asked her, did it make a big difference being on caffeinated coffee. I also asked her if she felt more awake and happier in the mornings?

She looked at me with a big smile on her face and told me that being back on caffeinated definitely made a difference and she felt much better.

She had no idea she was drinking decaf, but because she believed she was back on caffeinated coffee, she felt better!

It's important that you question everything, especially your beliefs about yourself, if you are talking to yourself negatively and subsequently running yourself down.

The more negative things you say to yourself, the more negative things are going to happen in your life.

However, if you talk positively to yourself you can change your results, achieve far more in life, and live a much happier and fulfilled life!

When I was terrible at running I told myself that I was a good runner.

Of course, I didn't tell anybody else this because it just wasn't true, but after telling myself how good a runner I was over-and-over in my mind, I eventually became quite good at running.

So, before you write yourself off, give yourself a chance and tell yourself that you are brilliant at what it is you want to be brilliant at!

YOUR DEFINITION OF SUCCESS

"Nothing can stop the man with the right mental attitude from achieving his goal; nothing on earth can help the man with the wrong mental attitude."
- Thomas Jefferson

This is without a doubt the shortest chapter in the book and I've made it that way for a specific reason.

It's short and sweet and I'm hoping it'll stick in your mind.

Ultimately, you have to know your own definition of success and everyone has their own definition of success.

Some people will define success in terms of money or fame.

Some people will define it as how many countries they've been to.

Some people define it as how much free time they have to do the things they love to do.

Some will define it as how fit or strong they are.

To some people, it's giving up alcohol or getting off drugs.

To some people it's being a great parent and for some people it's being given the 'all clear' when they've been battling a life threatening illness.

All of these things are success, but in broader terms, the best definition I've heard on success comes from Oscar winning actor

Anthony Hopkins in a great interview with former ITN newsreader Martyn Lewis for Martyn's book, 'Reflections on Success.'

"Success in relationship to me, my own personality is about conquest, triumphing over, overcoming. Overcoming adversities in oneself, limitations in oneself but also keeping a balance and I think a sense of humour about oneself, not making it the God but having a fair balance. That is it basically, in a few words...triumph, achievement, overcoming!"

Obviously, the words succeed, and success are closely related so let's take a look at the Cambridge dictionary to see how they define it:

'If you succeed, you achieve something you have been aiming for, and if a plan or a piece of work succeeds, it has the results that you wanted.'

In other words, know what you want out of life, follow your heart, and don't go chasing other people's definition of success!

KNOW WHAT YOU WANT

"The only person you are destined to become is the person you decide to be."

- Ralph Waldo Emerson

When it comes to getting what you want out of life everyone has different ideas of what they want most.

The people who I admired the most were the ones that were super fit.

For me, the one thing that I wanted to be the most was super fit, which was, at that point in my life, not very realistic as my fitness was extremely poor when I was 16 years old.

Becoming an Army Commando was the first step on the fitness ladder for me and if you would have offered me a choice between becoming an Army Commando and a million pounds I can say, with my hand on my heart it was to become a Commando. That's how bad I wanted it!

Fuck big houses, fuck supercars, fuck travelling around the world on a yacht, I wanted to be an Army Commando and nothing, but nothing was going to stop me getting that Green Beret!

When you are that passionate about something, you put massive effort in and have an unbelievable determination... it's very difficult to stop you.

If you were in 29 Commando Regiment you were already very fit compared to most people but as high as the standards were in 29, there were two guys who (in my mind) stood out from the rest of us.

Their names were Ian Marsh AKA 'Marshy,' and Brian Davidson AKA 'Beastie.'

They were the kind of people that were legendary in 29, they could do things that not only normal people couldn't do, they could do things that most high achievers and elite military soldiers couldn't do.

I was in 7 Battery and was based in Arbroath, Scotland.

Marshy was in 79 Battery in Plymouth and then went into 148 Battery based in Poole. And Beastie was in 7 Battery and later moved to HQ Battery in 29 Commando's main base...The Royal Citadel in Plymouth.

Marshy later transferred to the Physical Training (PT) Corps and flew through the tests to get into the PT Corps.

The Chief Instructor on Marshy's PT course was Glyn Sheppard who by coincidence, lived in my hometown of Haverfordwest.

Glyn said that he remembered Marshy doing the test for dips.

30

I didn't ask Glyn what the pass rate was; I just assumed it be about 10 to 20 dips. Marshy did 130 dips and was still powering on when Glyn told him to get off the bar as he had to move onto the next test because of time restrictions!

Glyn said that Marshy went on to break most of the PT Corps physical test records.

Beastie's main claim to fame was winning the West Highland Way Race 3 times!

The West Highland Way Race is one of the world's longest established ultra marathons which first took place in 1985 on the long-distance trail between Milngavie (just north of Glasgow) and Fort William in the Scottish highlands.

The race is 95 miles which includes 14,760 feet of ascent.

All competitors must complete the race within 35 hours and there are many failures even amongst some very fit people.

Two days before writing these words I was talking to a guy who was in the UK Special Forces (SF) that attempted the West Highland Way race.

To get into UK SF, there are many tough endurance challenges which are responsible for the majority of failures.

It is said that on average 90% of people who attempt SAS selection fail the course.

Compare this to a tough challenge such as the Ironman where most people who enter it get through the course and an average of only 10% of the people that enter it fail to complete it.

The former SF soldier humbly admitted that he attempted the notorious West Highland Way run and never made it to the end (although he did manage a very respectable 70 miles).

I respected him for not only taking on the ultra run, but for also having the honesty to admit it was too much for him.

Of course, completing a tough endurance challenge is one thing, but being one of the best, if not 'The Best' is a whole different ball game!

Amazingly while running the course, Beastie's main fuel was Mars bars and when he finished the 95-mile race he would always hit the pub for a pint...fucking legend!

I remember watching Beastie and Marshy break the military marathon world record which is a 26.2-mile speed march carrying 40lbs.

When Marshy and Beastie did the military marathon world record they were part of a 29 Commando team and could only go as fast as the slowest team member because it was a team record.

I remember looking at them both when they finished the challenge, to my surprise they both looked as if they had just gone for a walk in the park.

I thought that was super cool and wanted to be just like them, but it didn't happen overnight, and it wasn't until I'd left the army that my fitness level went to a completely different level!

Knowing what you really want may sound like an obvious thing, and many people who leave school don't know what they want, I know this because I was one of those people.

I've also met people in their 20's that don't really know what they want to do with their lives.

Sure they'd like to be successful, but they have no idea what they'd like to be successful at.

This goes back to the classic analogy where a person without a goal is like a ship without a rudder where the ship randomly sails from one place to another hoping that it will be lucky and find paradise.

It is possible that you could bump into a paradise island on your random voyage, but it's very unlikely and nowhere as certain as if you were using a GPS or a map and a compass.

A friend phoned me up one day and said that the next step for me is to get onto the TV and have my own chat show, as I've interviewed many high achievers on my YouTube Channel and it's a natural next step!

However, the truth is I'm not that interested in being famous.

Of course there are millions of people out there who would love to be famous and there are those people out there that will do anything they can (morally or not) just to get into a national newspaper, on TV or the radio.

I would be a hypocrite if I said I'd never go into any of those platforms as I've already been in them.

It was only to serve a purpose of getting my message out there on a bigger scale rather than the whole, "hey look at me, I'm in the national papers etc..." There was a time when I did want to get into the national papers but when I achieved that in my 20's the novelty wore off really quickly.

I remember talking to one of my mates who was a bodyguard for some of the most famous people on the planet.

He told me a story about one of the top A-list celebrities he looked after and said that one day after work he went to a bar, came back to the celeb's house and the celeb asked him what it was like going to the bar?

My mate said he was slightly taken back with the question at first and initially thought it was a strange question to ask; he told him it was nice and thought nothing of going into a bar for a quiet drink.

Of course, the A-lister wouldn't be able to walk into a bar without people bombarding him for selfies and autographs.

So there are always good things and bad things about certain levels of achievement and you ultimately have to ask yourself the question, "what is it you really want?" because you have to take the good with the bad.

For me I have several things that matter more to me than the rest. Number 1 on my list is to be the most successful Daddy I can be to my son Léon.

To excel at being the best Dad mainly comes down to how much time I spend with him and how much quality time he gets from me. With Léon mainly living with his Mum and Stepdad I don't get to see him everyday, but whenever I see him (usually every other weekend, every Tuesday after school and Wednesday morning when I drop him off to school) he knows that he is loved. There are always lots of cuddles and lots of me saying things like, "Love you Léon," and questions like, "do you know who your Daddy loves more than anyone else in the world?"

To which he always says "Me," and I reply, "that's right; your Daddy loves you more than anyone else in the world."

I also make sure that Léon has good manners and is kind to people. We can all influence other people; especially our children and they can often copy what we do.

The reason I am able to write a book on success is mainly due to my success in running but doing well in running is way down the list of importance for me compared to being an extremely successful Father.

You've always got to know what you want and if you're not getting closer to achieving your goal you may have to adjust, or you may have to keep going.

Not everything you put effort into works, but if you put effort into something you'll attract better results than you would without doing anything.

When there are roadblocks in life, it doesn't mean that you're not going to get to your main goals.

Just set goals and take action towards them, let go of the outcome and put the work in.

Will the work always pay off?

No, but at least you've tried, and you won't look back regretting that you never gave it a shot!

I was talking to a friend outside my house one day and he said that he couldn't run because he found it so boring, but at the same time he really wanted to lose weight.

I knew exactly how he felt as I remember going on the treadmill and doing a 10-minute run that I found very boring.

You may think that this was when I first started running, but it wasn't.

It was when I had already achieved many of my running goals and I had got out of the habit of doing consistent exercise.

The reason I found it so boring was because I had lost my 'why,' I had lost my purpose and I no longer had a strong enough reason to do it.

I had got comfortable and was no longer growing mentally.

My friend told me he was in a very dark place and he asked me if I could help him.

I explained to him I knew how he felt, and he said, "I'll give you a call sometime."

It is said that the road of 'sometime' leads to a destination called 'never.'

'Sometime' can lead to failure, but when you have a goal to do something in a certain time frame then you will be more focused, and you will get things done far faster!

When it came to write this book, I had no choice but to get on top of things. I had little time in the day to do things with everything else going on, but I had to make time.

The people that are the most productive and who achieve the most, often take on other projects and tasks even though they are already busy.

You can do far more than you think you can.

It's like weight training.

Many times people hit a plateau with the weight they are lifting.

You think you can only lift a certain weight but when you try something heavier you often find that you can lift more than you thought you could.

It's the same with running.

Many people have a peak of 26.2 miles - a marathon. They think that a marathon is the ultimate they could do, when in reality, a marathon is just a distance set up by some other human.

It's very important to always visualise yourself as being successful!

The chances are you have already been successful at many things. They don't need to be big things; a success is a success and you can build on that!

There are 'event' successes that don't happen very often such as a marathon or getting a diploma, which could take you years to achieve.
These long-term event successes are important.

However, an even more important success is the 'feeling' of being successful every day!

We need both in our lives, but we need that daily feeling of success and happiness the most because 'event' successes are here one moment and gone the next.

So when you want to feel successful and good about yourself, think back to some of the things that you've accomplished in your life.

Decide what you want to achieve and take action every day to achieve your goals!

SEEING WHAT OTHERS CANNOT

"Every block of stone has a statue inside it, and it is the task of the sculptor to discover it."

- Michelangelo

A few years ago, I travelled to Rome with my then girlfriend to see the sights - the Colosseum, the Vatican City, the Sistine Chapel, and many other beautiful sights that Rome has to offer.

One of the things we saw was Michelangelo's Pietà and statue of David, which is the one that is stark bollock naked with a little winky and is perhaps Michelangelo's most famous sculpture.

However, out of all of Michelangelo's sculptures it was the Pietà that impressed me the most.

It was mind-blowing to me to see the incredible detail that Michelangelo had put into this sculpture of Mary holding the body of Jesus.

I was amazed how from a block of marble this masterpiece was created!

Michelangelo also said (referring to his statue of an angel), "I saw the angel in the marble and carved until I set him free."

It's the same thing with us, we need to discover who we really are and chip away at our rough edges to reveal the greatness that lies inside us.

We may be underperforming in life and we're not becoming the person we know we could be.

We think we're average and sure enough by thinking we're average we stay average, but inside us there is infinite power, we are more than we may be showing, and like the great Michelangelo we must have a vision; a vision not just of what we are trying to achieve, but also a vision of the person we dream of becoming.

To make our dreams a reality, it'll take time and we have to use the best information, systems, contacts and training that we can.

Sometimes you'll enjoy the process and sometimes you won't!

What is true of every great achievement you'll make in your life is that it'll take a lot of effort to achieve your goals and your vision!

But to achieve your goals you need to chip away bit-by-bit, day-by-day.

This may be in the form of exercise, or a project you're working on.

With me, and this book, it's a case of doing things word-by-word, sentence-by-sentence, day-by-day and week-by-week.

If you're like me then you'll have days where you just can't be bothered to exercise, eat healthy, or do something that you know you should be doing.

Don't beat yourself up about it too much, all that matters is, "are you further ahead with your goals this year than you were last year?"

If you are, then good!

So, are you further ahead with your goals than you were last month?

If you are, great!

Are you further ahead with your goals this week than you were last week?

If you are, brilliant!

Sometimes we need to take a break, but if we want to achieve more and we've taken a 2 or 3 year break; then maybe it's time to brush the cobwebs off our dreams and bring them back into our life.

Many people only believe what they see; if they cannot see something they cannot believe it.

Years ago, people believed things that weren't true.

For example, most people believed that the world was flat!

When we look at the world and the sky it seems that the earth is not moving but in reality our planet is spinning at roughly 1,000 miles an hour, so just because your eyes can't see something it doesn't mean that it's not happening, or it can't happen.

In 1990, I left school and went out into the big wide world.

That very same year NASA launched the Space Shuttle Discovery, which carried the Hubble space telescope.

The Hubble was conceived in the 1940's and built in the 1980's.

What this tells us is that great dreams can take a while before they become a reality, so we have to look at the long term game plan!

We also have to be patient.

When you look at Hubble, it looks like a bunch of 6-year olds got together in a classroom with some cardboard from a toilet roll with tin foil and slapped the whole thing together, but no matter how it looks, the Hubble space telescope is a seriously awesome bit of kit!

The Hubble space telescope was built to see further than any other telescope so they launched it into space, which meant it couldn't be distorted with the effects of the Earth's atmosphere.

Much like the Earth's atmosphere that distorts telescopes from seeing what lies further; people also have distortions about how far they can really go.

In space, Hubble could see approximately 10-times further than telescopes on the ground.

When people look into space, all they can usually see is the blackness of space and stars but there is obviously far more out there than we can physically see.

Hubble can see everything from the formation of distant galaxies to the planets in the solar system.

The camera can see three different kinds of light such as near-ultraviolet, visible and near-infrared.

Just because, we can't see something, it doesn't mean it can't exist or it can't become a reality.

Many people won't be able to see your vision but if you have a dream you have to pursue it, because if you don't you'll end up being one of those people that has regrets and says things like, "if only I would have."

Have a vision of what you want, be willing to put the work in and go for it!

THE EXPERTS CAN BE

WRONG

*"First they ignore you, then they laugh at you, then they fight you,
then you win."*

- *Gandhi*

In my book 'The Underdog,' one of the chapters is called 'Standing on The Shoulders of Giants' which talks about learning off experts and people that have gone before.

While this is generally good practice, there are situations when even the experts get it wrong.

So it's important to keep an open mind and think carefully about people saying what is possible and what is not possible and make your own mind up.

Many of the things we learn and many of the questions we have in life have already been discovered and answered by someone else.

This may seem like a bit of a contradiction, and yes a lot of the time the experts will be right, but there are times when you want to do something that is beyond the vision of certain experts.

But who are experts?

There are 2 main types of experts:

1. **Bluffers - those that think they're experts and we initially think are experts but aren't.**
2. **Those that are experts but can, on occasion be wrong.**

Let's have a look at an example of the different type of experts:

1. Bluffers

One day I went up to my local sports shop to get some new running shoes. As I was sitting down one of the salespeople came up to me. He was dressed in sports kit and he asked me what I needed a new pair for.

I told him that I needed new sports shoes for running so without me saying any more on the subject he decided to give me his expert opinion.

He told me that the best thing that I could do was use a certain brand. As soon as he said the brand I thought it was a bit suspect because it wasn't a well-known brand in the running world.

He took me over to the place where it said 'running shoes' and I noticed that the brand he promoted had more types of running shoe on the rack than any other make displayed there.

I could smell a rat!

There were hardly any of the usual players such as Reebok, Asics, New Balance, Adidas, or Nike on the rack.

I then asked him if the company that he was working for also owned this particular make of shoe.

He told me that they did.

Bingo!

They were promoting their running shoe simply because they wanted not only to look better in the shop, but there would also be a considerable profit when they sold their running shoe.

In other words, the mark-up of the shoe from wholesale to retail was much greater, so it was all about profit rather than looking after the customer properly.

Nevertheless, the salesperson told me that these were still the best running shoes.

I don't go around telling everyone I bump into about my running experience because I don't want to sound like a twat and I simply don't feel the need to.

However, it had come to a head when I knew he didn't know what he was talking about and to be fair to him, he was probably told to tell customers that these are the best running shoes.

Trying not to sound like a dick, I told him about some of my running experience and then held the shoe he was promoting in my hand and told him why it wasn't a good running shoe.

It mainly boiled down to the shock absorption of this type of shoe.

I said to him, "No disrespect but can you get me the type of running shoe that I always use for running please?"

At this point he knew the game was up and he had to get me exactly what I wanted.

In other words, before you blindly listen to someone who labels himself or herself as 'an expert,' do some research first. We're lucky to live in a time where we can research topics and products on the Internet, so it's always good practice to research things before we believe what someone tells us.

2. Those that are experts but can, on occasion be wrong.

I first came across this when I was 17 years old and in the army. I was in Junior Leaders Regiment, Royal Artillery and my Sergeant Major asked me what regiment I would like to go into after I finish my training.

Even now I can clearly remember what happened.

My reply to this question was, "29 Commando Sir."

I'll never forget the look he gave me.

It was one of those looks as if to say, "There's no fucking chance you'll get into that regiment!"

Thank God he wasn't drinking anything when I told him; I think he would have spat it out.

In all fairness to him, he was a good guy and I think deep down he wished me all the best.

Right then and there I could have talked myself out of going for the Commando Course.

I could have said to myself, "Hey, this sergeant major is a great soldier with years of experience and if he doesn't think I'll pass this course, what's the point of even trying."

However, if we are to achieve our dreams, we must go after them, even if someone who we respect and who has a lot of credibility thinks we can't do it.

We may be wrong, but if we give it our best shot then we won't look back with regrets.

A great example of this is the Levi Roots story.

I had the pleasure of interviewing Levi after I saw him on the TV.

Levi had had a dream of selling his barbecue sauce on a national and international level.

He'd sold it for years locally and then decided to take a bold move and to go onto a BBC TV show called Dragons Den to see if he could get some millionaire investors to invest in his product to take his business further.

'Dragons Den' is a show in the UK and just like the TV show in the States called 'Shark Tank,' entrepreneurs pitch ideas to potential investors.

If the millionaire or millionaires like the entrepreneur's ideas they invest money and time in them.

When Levi walked into the room to pitch his product to the wealthy entrepreneurs, he was playing a guitar.

Obviously, this is not a conventional way to do a proposal to investors, but it did make him stand out.

Unfortunately, as he told the potential investors about his plans he completely messed up the sales figures, so things weren't looking good.

Three of the millionaires that Levi pitched to didn't believe it was going to work.

The first possible investor, Duncan Bannatyne said, "Levi there's no business in this, I'm not going to invest."

The second possible investor Deborah Meaden said, "I think you've got a great business but it's for you and you will do well out of it, it's not going to be on a big enough scale for me so I'm out."

The third possible investor, Theo Paphitis said, "It's a hugely complex difficult business getting to major supermarkets. In fact I'd go as far as to say, you've got very little hope, so I'm afraid Levi, I'm out."

At this point Levi was probably thinking, "Fuck!"

The fourth possible investor, Richard Farleigh thought Levi's business skills would need some help, but he liked Levi's charisma.

And the fifth possible investor, Peter Jones said, "We know how competitive this market is, it's almost impossible, I like impossible challenges."

When I interviewed Levi, we talked about his experience in the Dragons Den.
Levi went into the Dragons Den and asked for an investment of £50,000.
He eventually got the 50 grand off Peter and Richard for 40% of his company and they did make the so-called impossible possible.

Now 'Reggae Reggae Sauce' is in supermarkets all over the UK and Ireland. Sainsbury's were the first supermarket to take it on and expected the sauce to sell 50,000 bottles in its first year, but to their amazement it sold 40,000-50,000 bottles per week!
Levi also didn't do too bad and now has a net worth of tens of millions even though 3 experts said it would never happen!

Here are some other examples of experts not getting it right:

In 1878, a professor at Oxford University called Erasmus Wilson said, "When the Paris exhibition closes, the electric light will close with it and no more will be heard of it."
Professor Erasmus was a very clever man, but there are now billions of common light bulbs in use around the world.

In 1828, Dr Dionysius Larder, a science writer and academic made the case that "Rail travel at high speed is not possible because passengers would be unable to breathe."

Today, the Shanghai Maglev Train reaches 268 mph during its daily service.

In 1876, senior executives at Western Union said, "This telephone has too many shortcomings to be seriously considered as a means of communication. It is inherently of no value."

According to staissta.com, in 2019 there were 931 million fixed telephone lines.

According to IHS Markit, in 2019 Apple shipped 193 million smartphones and Samsung shipped over 100 million more at 295 million!

And that's not to mention all of the other phone makes around the world.

Not including landlines, it is estimated that over 17 billion mobile phones have been sold since they were first introduced.

In 1895, Lord Kelvin, president of the Royal Society of Science, expertly argued that "Heavier-than-air flying machines are impossible."

But on 17 December 1903, the Wright brothers proved him wrong by inventing, building, and flying the world's first airplane.

In 1899, Charles H. Duell, Commissioner of the US Office of Patents said that "Everything that can be invented has been invented."

Since then more than, 7 million inventors have received patents from the US Patent office.

In 1903, Horace Rackham, the president of the Michigan Savings Bank advised Henry Ford's own lawyer not to invest in the Ford Motor Company.

He said, "The horse is here to stay, and the automobile is only a novelty."

According to worldometers.info, there are now over 1 billion cars worldwide!

In 1936, editors at the New York Times wrote, "A rocket will never leave Earth's atmosphere." Just 6 years later, the V2 missile, which was first launched by Germany, made it into space.

Less than 15 years after that, the Russians launched a rocket with the first satellite ''Sputnik', into space.

In 1943, Thomas Watson, chairman of IBM said, "I think there is a world market for maybe five computers."

There are now over 2 billion computers connected to the Internet, which accounts for roughly 28% of the global population (at the time of writing).

In 1946, Darryl Zanuck, the founder of 20th Century Movie Studio and winner of 3 Academy Awards said, "Television won't last because people will soon get tired of staring at a plywood box every night."

Now, billions of hours of TV are watched each day from people all over the world.

In 1954, Dr. Wilhelm Hueper, Director of the National Cancer Institute, argued that, "If excessive smoking actually plays a role in the production of lung cancer, it seems to be a minor one."

According to tobaccoatlas.org, tobacco use has killed 100 million people in the 20th century, which is more than all of the deaths in World War 1 and World War 2 combined!

In 1959, IBM reported to the future founders of Xerox "The world potential market for copying machines is 5,000 at most."

While the photocopier is expected to become obsolete by many people, Xerox generated over $18.2 billion in copier sales, managing 60 billion printed pages.

In 1968, Time Magazine made the observation that, "Online shopping, while entirely feasible, will flop."

In 2013, worldwide online shopping reached nearly $1 trillion. At the time of writing, Goldman Sachs predicts year-over-year growth of almost 20% and life for me along with many of us wouldn't be the same without Amazon.

In 1969, Margaret Thatcher told an audience, "It will be years, not in my lifetime, before a woman becomes Prime Minister."

Ten years later she would prove her own prediction wrong by winning the 1979 UK general election.

In 1981, Bill Gates, founder of Microsoft prophesied the maximum speed of computers.

In his opinion he thought that 640K ought to be enough for anybody. Today, the average personal computer is 300 million times faster than that.

In 1987, long-serving TV weather forecaster Michael Fish said that the BBC had received a phone call from a lady saying, "I hear there's a hurricane on the way."

Fish confidently told the British public, "Don't worry, there isn't."

No prizes for guessing what happened next!

MADE OF THE WRIGHT
STUFF

"The moment you doubt whether you can fly, you cease forever to
be able to do it."
- *J.M. Barrie (Author of Peter Pan)*

At the time of writing these words, I consider myself incredibly lucky to have travelled to 56 countries around the world.

For most of these journeys I flew by aeroplane, as millions of people have done. Today, we take the aeroplane for granted and even since the very day I was born the aeroplane was already in production, so to me it was just part of the society and part of the world I grew up in.

However, it wasn't always this way.

When people first had the idea of flying they come across huge criticism from others.

First of all, there was the subject of weight.

How could something that weighed a lot more than a feather possibly fly around in the sky?

Surely, this was impossible?

Today, the average aeroplane weighs several tonnes, but fly they do!

Two brothers from Ohio had a dream of flying.

However, despite having good reputations for being kind and helpful people, when the public found out about their idea to build a machine that could fly, well let's just say many people thought the two brothers had lost the plot!

Neither of the brothers had finished high school but both brothers were skilled mechanics.

At this time people around the world were building gliders and were trying to fly.

The most famous person was the German Otto Lilienthal, who had experimented with over 2000 glider flights, but sadly one day in 1896 he crashed and died; his death made international headlines.

When the two brothers saw this they thought to themselves, well maybe we can create something that can fly?

The two brothers thought the best thing to do was to be able to control a glider.

Having already done a lot of work with bicycles they knew about controlling motion and their own research found that to fly aeroplane it would need to be controlled in three separate axes:

• Pitch (i.e. nose up or nose down)

• Yaw (i.e. left or right)

• Roll (i.e. rotates left or right)

Arguably, the most difficult to control of these three was the roll, so what the brothers did was study birds.

Birds are obviously the masters of flying, so it made sense to study how they moved.

This is no different when we want to achieve big things in our own lives.

We need to look at who has mastered what we want to do and emulate them!

The brothers noticed that birds change the angle of their wingtips to create a lateral motion, which is known as wing warping.

For the birds it obviously comes naturally, but the challenge was how would they put wing warping into one of their machines?

The eureka moment came to them one day when the brothers were working at their bicycle shop and a young boy came in and asked for an inner tube for his bike.

When one of the brothers pulled out the end of tube from the cardboard box that it came in, it gave him an idea of how the long flap-lidded box design could be used on a flying machine to deliver what they termed 'wing warping'.

They needed to build a glider with movable parts on the wings that could be altered to change its geometry, and thus, increase or decrease the lift that was needed.

For several years they experimented with small model gliders and then decided to build a glider that was big enough to carry a man. By initially doing things on a small scale, this meant that the project costs were minimal, and when they had to adjust things and more importantly get airborne themselves, they would be less likely to get killed!

With our dreams and goals we often have to start off small.

If you started a fitness regime then you probably began by running only one or two miles rather than going out for a 10-miler at your first attempt.

It's a good thing to stretch ourselves but we also need to be careful that we don't risk too much, too soon and consequently crash and burn!

If you push your fitness too hard and too fast then there is a good chance you're going to come away with an injury and you're going to feel pretty negative about the whole experience.

It always makes sense to start small.

It's the same for when I started writing; I was over the moon if I could write 200 words in one day!

I could have never imagined that I would eventually get to a stage where I was consistently banging out over 3000 words-a-day, and sometimes up to 7000 words. So, set your goals small and then build on them!

In 1901, the brothers decided to test the glider and were willing to travel to wherever to pursue their joint dream as they needed a location that would provide strong and steady winds to increase the lift of the glider.

They came to the conclusion that Kitty Hawk in North Carolina was the very place they needed to be.

I have found that a willingness to go anywhere to further a project or yourself is something that is common with successful people.

They are not afraid to go to where they need to go to achieve the success they want to achieve.

You've got to be willing to get out there in the world, that way you'll come across many more opportunities than you would if you stayed in your local area!

Not only is travel important for success, I also believe that it's important to expand your mind and subsequently gain a worldly view.

You may not have to go up over 100 feet in the air to make your dreams come true, but the chances are you will need some bravery to a certain extent.

Anything that we believe in and want to pursue does require a certain amount of courage.

If you're a bit like me, you may not know exactly what you're doing when you start out on a new adventure, but sometimes it's just a case of experimenting and fumbling through until you get it right.

The good news here is the chances are if you make mistakes while pursuing your dream, you won't be killed like the brothers would have been.

Your ego maybe a little bit bruised, but all you need to do is pick yourself back up and keep on moving forward!

When they experimented with their first glider, the brothers thought that would be the day they would solve the problem of wing warping and could fly like a bird, unfortunately, it didn't work out that way. Another problem that they had was they couldn't create enough lift for the glider; and on top of that, one of the brothers was almost killed!

They almost quit the entire project but didn't!

When I started my quest to become an author, I can honestly say that there were times when I wanted to quit and never write another word!

However, with hindsight I can now look back at those early days and clearly see that I just wasn't committed, which is kind of like giving up without saying that you've actually quit.

If I wasn't putting words down towards a new book, or editing what I had already wrote, then I wasn't getting any closer to producing a new book.

So if you're not taking action towards your dreams, nothing will change for you!

The brothers eventually fixed the wing warping challenge by replacing the rudder and then decided to build their own wind tunnel, which was a box about 6-foot long with a fan at one end that blew air into the box.

As I type these words, I'm thinking about how much the brothers got paid while doing their experiments.

The reality was, they had no big corporation giving them huge amounts of money, and they were just funding the project by the proceeds that they would make from their bicycle shop!

That's the same as many successful people.

They don't start off with a huge pot of cash and many people on their team helping them, they start off very small and build upon that.

Once you start producing results and people see that you're committed, then more people will support you and want to help you achieve your dreams.

Some people will need to be paid and some people will be inspired by what you do and just want to help out.

When I decided to commit fully to producing my first book 'The Underdog', I wasn't working as much as I could have worked, and the only work I did was to cover the bills.

Of course while I was writing I wasn't getting paid to write, but I didn't care because my dream was to become an author and that is what inspired me.

The brothers spent several months testing out different wing shapes to see which wing shape would be the best for lift.

After conducting lots of tests, they discovered that if they made the wing thicker at the front and thinner at the back it decreased pressure above the wing and increased the pressure below the wing, which would create lift.

In 1902, the brothers went back to Kitty Hawk to test the new prototype.

There were doubts but the glider worked brilliantly…it was a massive breakthrough!

One year later, they designed a glider with a petrol engine and they optimistically called the glider (with an engine) 'The flyer.'

The glider was made in their bike shop and they also designed the bespoke wooden propellers.

On 17th December 1903, a crowd of people watched in amazement as Orville Wright flew the first motorised plane!

The flight was only 12 seconds long, but those 12 seconds were so significant it changed the history of the world!

The brothers then flew an additional three flights with a combined time of roughly 60 seconds.

When the Wright Brothers built their first glider in 1900, the wingspan was 17ft 6in (5.33m). Its length was 11ft 9in (3.51m) and it weighed 52lbs (24kg).

I don't think even the Wright brothers would've believed that in 1988 an aircraft called Mriya and given the designation An-225 by Antonov (a Ukrainian aircraft manufacturer) would be built with the following specifications: wingspan 290ft (88.4m), length 275ft 7in (84m) and weight without fuel 628,317lbs (285,000kg or 314.158 tons).

It could also carry a payload of 545,000lbs (247,000 kg) in a commercial flight.

As you've probably already guessed the Mriya is the largest aeroplane in the world and also the heaviest aircraft ever that's ever flown.

I'm sure the brothers would also be interested to know that the official record for the fastest aeroplane in the world at the time of writing is still the Lockheed SR-71 Blackbird, which was recorded at 2,193 mph (3,530 kph) on the 28th July 1976.

Ever so slightly faster than the 19.1mph that Wilbur Wright recorded on the 14th December 1903 at Kitty Hawk.

According to the Daily Telegraph, in 2017 commercial aircraft carried nearly 4 billion passengers according to the International Air transport Association (That number represents individual journeys rather than unique passengers), which is nearly twice as many individual flights as there were 12-years ago!

Nobody has an exact figure for how many aeroplanes there are in the world today. Although, according to Ascend, who do aviation analysis, they estimate that there are roughly 23,600 aircraft currently in service with 2,500 in storage. The online publication Airliners.net estimates that there are even more. They estimate that there are around 39,000 planes in the world and throughout the history of the world there have been more than 150,000 planes!
The International Civil Aviation Organisation has said that the global air transport network doubles in size every 15 years.

At the time of editing this book, the COVID-19 virus is sweeping through the world and the airline industry has been severely affected.
However, it is widely believed that most of us will get through this and get back to normal life.

Whatever happens in the world from now on there is absolutely no doubt...Orville and Wilber Wright changed history when they invented the aeroplane.

So what were the lessons that we can learn from these incredible brothers?

- **Follow your dreams.**

- **Dream big.**

- **Don't listen to people who think you're crazy.**

- **If you didn't excel in school it doesn't matter. You can still achieve great things.**

- **Look at what someone else has done, learn from it and create something better.**

- **Shine in your chosen field by putting lots of time and effort into it.**

- **Look for opportunities in everyday life to achieve your goals.**

- **Start small and build on that.**

- **Be willing to travel to make your dreams come true.**

- **Take risks.**

- Experiment with new ways.

- You will always make some mistakes.

- Things that you first thought would work may not work.

- If you fail, pick yourself up and keep going.

- Be committed.

- Don't quit, even when the going is tough.

- Take action.

- Use what resources you've got and make the most of what you have.

- If you persist you will eventually get a breakthrough.

- Doubts are natural sometimes – push through them.

- Be optimistic, believe in yourself and believe in your dreams!

TAKE ACTION

"Success seems to be connected with action. Successful people keep moving. They make mistakes, but they don't quit."
- Conrad Hilton (Founder of Hilton Hotels)

Action will always beat inaction!

Every time you don't take action towards something you want to achieve; you are slowly failing in life!

This can be all-sorts of things from asking a girl or guy out on a date, to getting sponsorship for an event you're planning, or writing your book.

Sometimes you may think that people who are happy and have a great life have nothing challenging happen in their lives.

It may look like it on the outside but all of us have challenges, and in many cases, people who live a successful happy life have more challenges than the average person when it comes to achieving goals.

They have often been criticised more, failed more, and put their neck on the line more than most people.

If you lose at something then try your best to take it on the chin, accept it with humility and don't beat yourself up about it all day long.

You are mainly in competition with yourself anyway and as I've said before, the greatest battles are our battles of the mind.

One person who always took massive action was Dame Barbara Cartland.

Her first book called Jigsaw was published in 1925 when she was only 24 years old.

Barbara Cartland had an incredible book producing system.

She first lay down on a sofa with her little dog and her secretary was placed to the right slightly behind her.

When she was ready Barbara would start talking. Her secretary would take shorthand notes of everything Barbara was saying, and the notes would later be written into a book.

There was also a tape recorder so not one word was missed.

Barbara would start talking at 1:30pm every day just after lunch.

She was extremely punctual, and she believed that it was vital to start not at 1:35 PM or 1:40 PM but spot on 1:30 PM.

Along with her secretary, she was capable of producing 8000 words within the space of two hours.

While we are taking action and moving forward we always have a barrage of people giving us different types of advice.

Some advice is good, some advice not so good but ultimately when we push forward with things and see we've made a mistake, we can always adjust.

One of Barbara's policies was to have a happy ending in all of her books.

Her son said that she did produce one book that didn't have a happy ending and it was a complete disaster.

When the fans read the unhappy ending they sent Barbara letters from all over the world asking Barbara if 'Amy' - the main female character could marry the male hero at the end of the book instead of them being separated.

Barbara took her fans advice, changed the ending to a happy ending, which delighted her fans and they continued to buy her books in the millions.

The incredible thing about Barbara Cartland was even though she was so prolific with producing books; she was also a brilliant mother!

In other words, she always found time for her children.

In the morning she spent time with her children, in the afternoon she worked on her books and after she had finished working on her books she would spend teatime (around 5pm) with her children.

Barbara always used to say, "If you want to get something done then ask a busy person because they will get it done."

One of the things that I loved learning about Barbara Cartland was she was incredibly efficient with time.

After her secretary had written down Barbara's words, Barbara had 10 secretaries working with her reading, typing, and doing several other jobs.

She was interviewed on her 76th birthday and asked, "Why do you still produce books?"

There is no doubt that Barbara didn't need to do any more books, but she loved creating books and felt that what she was doing was worthwhile and other people enjoyed what she was producing.

Barbara's mother told her when she was younger, "When you grow up, you've got to do something in the world, you've got to give something, and you've got improve the world somehow."

Barbara said that when she produced lots of books she was criticised, and people would tell her that she did too many.

Some people said that they just don't want her books, which is fair enough, as different people want different things.

Nevertheless, she kept on taking action and produced 20 books in 1975, 21 books in 1976 and the year after it was 24 books.

According to her son, he doesn't think his father read any of his mother's books, which goes to show just because your partner isn't involved in your career; it doesn't mean they love you any less.

Barbara Cartland believed her vitamins contributed massively to her output and productivity.

She was also a fan of what was called back then, 'The health movement' and was a huge advocate of ginseng and vitamin B12.

Barbara Cartland was one of the most prolific and commercially successful authors in history!

She produced 723 novels, which were translated into 38 different languages.

In 1991, Queen Elizabeth II gave her the honour of becoming a Dame due to over 60 years of contributions towards society.

Many sources believe that she sold over 1 billion books!

The only authors to top this are William Shakespeare and Agatha Christie.

On 21 May 2000, at the age of 98 Barbara Cartland passed away at her residence in Hertfordshire, but she lived her dreams and died a happy, fulfilled woman.

She was a super-achiever, not only as an author, but, arguably even more importantly, as a parent, and that all boiled down to taking massive focused action!

More recently on 25 October 1984, a baby by the name of Catherine was born in Santa Barbara, California and was brought up by two loving parents who were Born-Again Christians.

From the age 3 to 11 years old, Catherine moved across the country as her parents set up churches where she also attended religious schools and camps.

She listened to gospel music and began to take singing lessons at the age of 9 where she started singing at a local church.

She also briefly studied Italian opera singing.

She loved music, started writing songs and started to play the guitar.

Catherine was taking massive action; she produced her first album, which sold 200 copies.

It wasn't going to set the world on fire, but she had achieved something she had never achieved before by producing the album.

Catherine was signed to two major record labels but was dropped by both.

Initially the record label didn't want her to come out with a song she loved. The reason for this was because they thought it was a bit risky and a bit too sexual.

As you can imagine her parents weren't fans of this either but in 2008 she released the song, which was called 'I kissed a girl' and it was a huge success!

She changed her name from Catherine Hudson because she didn't want to get confused with the actress Kate Hudson and became Katy Perry.

The rest as they say is history!

Catherine AKA Katy Perry became the first female artist to produce five number one Billboard hot 100 songs and she became Forbes top female earning artist for three years in a row.

How did she do it?

She took massive action!

She not only acted when things were going right for her, she also took action when things weren't going right for her.

So whatever is happening in your life, take action towards your goals!

Act when things are going well, take action when times are hard and even take action when all hell is breaking loose...just take action, action, and more action!

I was at the scooter park with my son Léon one day and another child said to his mum out loud in front of everyone, "you suck!" His mum just stood there and took it on the chin.

I felt a little sorry for this mother, but I didn't think she was handling the situation particularly well, so I said to her, "One of the best things I did in regards to bringing up my son was watching Super-nanny and Nanny 911. The people on these TV shows have had decades of experience in dealing with children with challenging behaviour. They had also achieved amazing results and have helped thousands of parents to get a loving more respectful household."

I told the mother of this rude child, If my son said that to me, I would give him a warning and say, "if you say that again to me you will be taken from the scooter park and lose the use of your scooter for at least 2 weeks!"

The mother said, "Yeah 'I SHOULD' watch that Super-nanny."

Watching or listening to something is one thing and taking action on it is quite another, but of course you know when someone says, 'I SHOULD' you know that chances are they won't do it.

Maybe you've done this in your own life where you say, 'I SHOULD' because you think it will help change the quality of your life, but you don't follow through and take action.

Saying 'I should' is admitting there is a problem and you're not actively working on the problem.

What you say when you talk to yourself massively affects the actions you take!

When you catch yourself saying, 'I SHOULD,' turn it into 'I WILL' and then
'I DO' or 'I'M DOING!'

'SHOULD' is weak, 'SHOULD' is mediocre, 'SHOULD' or 'I NEED TO' is what holds you back and makes you lose out on your dreams in life!

That sort of thinking is only one level above 'I CAN'T!'

It's much easier to take action when you used the words 'I AM.'

For example:

I AM FIT

I AM A HEALTHY EATER

I AM A GREAT PARENT

I AM BRILLIANT AT MY JOB

I AM VERY STRONG MENTALLY

I AM A WINNER

Of course it's no good just saying these things and not backing these things up with the research and finding out how other people have been successful in their chosen field.

By learning the techniques used by successful people it will give you more confidence, and when you join the acquired knowledge with your new positive self talk you will take a lot more action and become much more successful!

Yes you have to override some of your old conditioning and let go of the past that you've been holding onto, but if you want to create new and exciting changes in your life, you have to think differently and do differently!

Most of us want a great quality of life.

If you want to create the life you want then you have to be willing to put the effort in to get the great results.

If we see someone putting a lot of effort in, one of the expressions we use in the UK is… "He or she is a grafter!" meaning they are hardworking!

"If you want to create your dream life then you have to graft like fuck!"

One of the things that has been thrown around a lot in the last few years in the world of self-development is that successful people differ from the average person as they are willing to put in the amount of hours that is needed to become really good at something. It has been said that to really excel in something you must put in over 10,000-hours into your chosen field.

I don't know how many hours I put in to running but what I do know is that I've put in more time and hours into running than most of the people I know.

For some people, running a marathon is a lifelong ambition, it's one of those things that many people do along with skydiving to tick off their bucket list.

Many people will read a magazine article that gives advice about running a half marathon or a marathon and take the advice from the person writing the article in that magazine.

A new marathon runner (or some that aren't so new) will train by taking the advice of running magazine articles but many writers give out a training program that makes the would be marathoner under-train and just get through the marathon rather than complete the marathon in a good personal time.

I guess a good time is all relative and just running a marathon is a great achievement for many people, but the reality is very often people can complete a marathon a lot faster and a lot more efficiently if they put more hours in.

If you're looking for a sub four-hour marathon then you could get away with a running 30 to 40 miles a week.

However, if you want to get a better time then you're generally going to have to put more hours in!

When you look at the elite marathon runners, they are averaging 100 – 120 miles a week.

Of course we're not all elite marathon runners, we don't all weigh nine-and-a-half stone (134lbs) like running legend Haile Gebrselassie and we haven't all got incredible genetics.

However, can most people run 100 – 120 miles a week?

Absolutely!

Of course, no two people are the same and sometimes people get injured, or if they've just started running they won't be able to put in 100 - 120 miles a week.

That said, even if you put in 120 miles a week it doesn't mean you'll achieve a 2 hour 10 minute marathon like the elite runners, but what you will do is bring your time down quite considerably!

This is because your body is used to putting in the miles, but it's not only your body, your mind is far more used to it too!

On the flip side of that, when Ron Hill (who was the second man to break the time of 2 hours 10 minutes in a marathon) went over 120 miles a week in training, his marathon time was slower.

It has also been said that ultra-distance world record holder Yiannis Kouros trains no more that 80 miles a week.

So, where are the black and white statistics?

Surely, there should be a specific road map to the perfect training to get the best performance, right?

Well you would think so, but after much research on what makes the best the best, it seems that there is no one path to success!

Ultimately, you must listen to your body and if you constantly feel tired and drained then you'll need to take a rest, even if it's just for a day or two.

The same applies to work. If you feel mentally exhausted then you need to step back and go at a slower pace or take some time off work if that's possible.

So to summarise, 9 times out of 10 you will always get better results if you put more time into something, but at the same time you have to experiment with this and listen to your own body and mind.

FOCUS AND ADJUST

"Your life is controlled by what you focus on."

- Tony Robbins

In the year 2000, I decided to do a run in the United States taking in some great places and some iconic views.

The plan of action was to fly from the UK to Denver, Colorado and to start my run there.

When the plane landed, I got off, went through customs, walked outside the airport, made my way to a certain point in Denver and started running.

I hadn't slept much on the plane, but I wanted to start as soon as I could and didn't start running until late in the afternoon.

When I started running from Denver I had a goal to run 26 miles unsupported with a backpack weighing 45lbs.

I was carrying, spare clothes, my tent, a sleeping bag, wash kit, a gas cooker, dry food rations and lots of water.

I had carried this type of weight and heavier in my Army Commando days but there wasn't any consistent running so on the Commando Course it was at a much slower pace and usually a lot less miles were involved.

This challenge in the States involved much bigger distances and was tougher but I had matured, and my endurance was far stronger than when I did the Commando Course.

I didn't take into account that Denver 'the mile high city' had less oxygen than my home back in Cardiff, Wales.

I also thought that coming from Wales, I would be well prepared for the hills in the Rocky Mountains, but the Rockies were on a different level and were tougher!

The combination of weight on my back, having less oxygen than normal and the hills took its toll on my body.

I was falling behind with my goal of running 26-miles a day and every day I fell further behind with my miles, which meant things were compounding over time.

Being behind just a few miles every day would eventually mean that by the end I would be hundreds of miles behind schedule and quite some distance off my original goal, which was 2,000 miles.

After only 3 days of running and carrying the 45 lbs I was having trouble with my ankles, they were hurting, and I was at risk of pulling out of my 60 day run after only 3 days!

Running 26 miles at my own pace was usually fairly easy and carrying a pack doing a speed march (a combination between jogging and walking fast) would have been ok, but the problem was the consistent pounding effect from running continuously up and down hills carrying the 45lbs.

On the 3rd day I had to make a decision on what to do, I knew if this carried on I would probably pick up an injury.

I had featured in the national newspapers, I had been sponsored with the flights to fly over to the States, I had planned, I had trained, I had prepared and the last thing I wanted was to get only three or four days into a 60 day challenge and have to fly home.

I wanted to keep my dried food I brought to the States, as I only had $150 to last me two months but the food and cooker added another 10lbs to my pack. I was down to the bare essentials, but I needed the rest of my kit and most importantly the water.

In the end the food and the cooker was the only thing I could get rid of, so I dumped them, if I didn't adjust and focus on how to get through the run I would have never made it.

I was stuck in another country for 60-days and I only had $150 in my pocket, which I knew wasn't going to get me very far. I blew through the $150 within the first week so I needed to adjust my strategy to get through the next seven weeks and focus on a solution to get food.

I was burning thousands of calories a day, so it was vital to get food inside me otherwise my energy levels would be depleted, and I would fail.

I ended up going into anywhere that sold food and asked to see the Manager, where I would produce an article of me doing this charity run in one of the national newspapers.

I'd say something like, "Hi I'm doing a sponsored run for charity across part of the United States, is there any chance you can sponsor me a Big Mac meal please?" Nine times out of ten I'd get food and that's how I got through the whole run.

Some people may have been mentally paralysed and wondering what the hell they were going to do with being stuck in a foreign country for nearly 2 months without any money or food.

This just goes to show that you must focus and adjust with whatever life throws at you.

It's no good sitting on your hands and bitching about what isn't going right in your life.

If there's a problem, there is almost always a solution, so it's vital to focus on your goal, adjust when circumstances change, and move forward!

In the end I got through the run, even after being bedded down for 3-days with a nasty case of the flu.

Because of the timeframe I had, I didn't do the 2,000 miles I'd hoped to do but I did cover 1,620 miles, which was far better than anything I had done previously.

My friend Dai Llewellin is a multiple British Rally Driving Champion and has beaten some of the top rally drivers in the world.

When he is racing around a course do you think he's focused on a wall, a tree, a hedge or is he focused on where he's going next?

The answer is obvious but how many of us focus on the negative things?

In other words, if your focus is on bad things then guess where you're heading next?

Yep, you guessed it, a little town in your mind called 'Shitsville!'

We all have challenges in life, and we all have things that go wrong, but ultimately we need to get back on track by focusing on positive things and our destination!

Memories can be either unpleasant or nice to look back on.
For those people reading this that aren't on Facebook there is a feature on there called 'Facebook Memories' which lets you know what post you put up one year ago, two years ago, or however many years ago that you posted.
One day I saw a post I put that said:

"Wrote seven pages towards my new book last night, I think I can really get into this writing game. I'm also reading Phyllis Oostermeijer 'Choose Life' book!"

I was inspired by Phyllis, who is a local author and it made me think if a local living in my hometown can bring a book out, then so can I.
I'd thought about bringing a book out for years and had written some words many years before but I neither acted upon it nor pushed things forward!
So this was it, this was the start of me becoming a writing-machine and producing lots of books, right?
Wrong!

My first book 'The Underdog' was released in early 2017.

So why did it take over three and a half years for me to get my 1st book out?

One of the challenges was at the time it wasn't something that I really wanted to do. Of course it would be so cool to be an author and it would be even cooler to have a whole load of books out and supercool to be making a shit tonne of cash out of it!

I was struggling so much with writing that I needed to devise a new type of plan so I could get the words down and follow my dream of becoming a successful writer.

I needed to adjust and focus!

There are so many times during the day when other things would catch my attention and it would be easy to get distracted from writing.

Much of the time I'd rather be doing something else other than writing, as writing wasn't exactly my dream back then but having more of my books out was.

It was the same with my running, because I'm lucky enough to have two legs I do take it for granted and I have to say that while I am running I don't always enjoy it 100% of the time; but I do enjoy the feeling I get when I've completed a run and I enjoy the results it gets me.

I've also noticed that even though I hated running to begin with, I do enjoy the process now and it became that way with writing.

One of the things that I decided to do was to put my dream in front of me.

Many authors write the book and get the front cover designed when the book is finished.

Personally, I find it much better when I can see the book cover in front of me, and then I have a goal to work towards.

I start looking around for things that could go on the front cover of the book and I start to use applications such as the poster maker app on Android to create a rough design myself.

After this, I give it to my designer Tom, who is a bit of a whizz-kid on the Mac and Tom tidies things up for me to make them look better.

After going through a few different colours and images I will decide on the final image and Tom will send me the finished design.

The reason I had these cover prints was that I could focus better and work towards completing these books.

The danger was if I didn't have the goal in front of me every day, then I could easily slip into putting it off, and it was for this very reason that my first book, 'The Underdog' took me over three years to complete.

I would routinely lose focus and many times, lose interest in writing the book.

I would drift off, do other things and by doing this I would go months and sometimes years without achieving goals!

The other thing I started to do recently is to have a certain photo of my son Léon in front of me.

The reason for this is because Léon is my biggest supporter and my greatest reason for writing.

More published books equals more inspiration for Léon and also more money, which helps us have a better quality of life.

He also asks me about my progress with my books and it was too disappointing telling him I hadn't done anything.

I knew I had to lead by example!

So whether I'm home, on a train travelling or if I'm in a hotel room, I've got his photo in front of me to remind me:

1. How lucky I am to have him.
2. That I need to focus and take action so I can create a better future for him.

Starting something off can be difficult at first but the more you do of something the easier it becomes.

I knew that because I produced one book I was capable of producing another, and if I was capable of producing two books then I was capable of producing three, and so on.

You've probably had something like this in your own life when you've achieved a goal and by achieving that goal you had more belief to achieve your next goal.

Of course when you achieve one goal you would be more likely to put the effort into achieving your next goal.

The phrase 'success breeds success' is true!

What I needed to remember was the reason why I was writing.

I needed to produce more books, to not only make my dreams and my son's dreams come true by making more money, but to help other people with their own specific path in life.

You need to write down your own dreams and goals and take massive action, because when you do this they are more likely to become a reality!

It's also a good idea to get people to help you with your goals. When you've got a trainer or coach it can be of added benefit, because you're accountable to somebody, whereas if you just write your own goals down and don't tell other people and enlist help, you're only accountable to yourself!

Ultimately, everyone approaches things in their own unique way.

If something is not working for you, acknowledge what isn't working, focus on where you want to go, adjust what you are doing and take action!

HABITS

"Successful people are simply those with successful habits."

- Brian Tracy

Most people don't realise how important habits are.

Everything you ever achieve will be based on your habits!

Habits can seem insignificant and you may think that they don't make much of a difference, but the habits you do every day will have a massive effect on how your life turns out!

Even if you have a lot of willpower, it alone is not enough to get you to reach your biggest goals in life.

Willpower is most important in the early stages of working towards your goal but when you combine willpower with habit, that's when your life can change!

In my first book 'The Underdog' I talk about the wires and the steel cables on a suspension bridge and related those linkages to your mental strength.

You can also relate the steel wires to habits.

The more you do those little daily habits the more they become like the little steel wires bonded together on a suspension bridge, which then turn into one large cable to create something magnificent.

Habits will lead you in a certain direction whether you are aware of your habits or not.

They can cause you to miss out on the good things in life, they can bring you misery and bad health problems, or they can lead to a better, happier, and more fulfilled life.

If you run most days you may not be lucky enough to break a world record, but I can guarantee that you'll be far fitter than if you did nothing!

So doing nothing and being lazy is also a habit.

If you smoke every day, you may not get lung cancer, but I can guarantee your health will be worse and your clothes and breath won't smell as nice.

If you lift weights every week, you may not become Mr. Universe, but you will be stronger and healthier than if you didn't lift.

If you eat lots of junk food and sweets every day, you may not die from a heart attack but it's far more likely you will put on weight and develop health issues.

Your daily habits create big results in your life and it's up to you to decide if those habits lead you to a positive or a negative result.

When I started interviewing successful people, that idea came from an initial step where I first asked someone for an interview, and then, I developed a habit of messaging someone new once a week. Having messaged someone new twice a week, it then became once every two days, then I got to the stage where I thought I'd send out 2-messages per day and see what results I get back.

One day I sent over 30 tweets to high achievers.

I also got into the habit of looking for events that I could go to and find cool new people that I wanted to interview.

Did these habits bring results?

You bet!

You only have to type my name into YouTube or go onto my Facebook 'Mark Llewhellin Tips On Success Coaching' page to see what results these habits brought in.

It's also worth mentioning that I've created another chapter in this book, which is called, 'If You Don't Ask' and specifically applies to how I ended up interviewing so many successful people.

There are many different factors when it comes down to being successful, but I can't promote enough that one of the very biggest keys to succeeding is down to your habits.

Training once or twice a week is usually harder for most people than training 4 - 6 days a week.

Why?

Because when you train at least 4 days a week it becomes a habit.

It's just part of your daily routine.

It's who you are, it's what you do and it's part of your identity as a person.

You can often tell who's training and who isn't just by looking at them when they're wearing clothes that complement their body.

They put the effort in, they stand out, they look good and they feel better for it.

When it comes to daily tasks like walking up a set of stairs it's easier for them because they've done the cardio in the gym, in the hills or out on the road.

When they carry the shopping bags, it's easier for them because they've been lifting weights almost every day in the gym.

Of course you can get overweight people that train on a consistent basis too, but the main reason that they would be overweight is because of what they put in their mouth!

If you want to better control your eating habits then you've got to give yourself a good enough reason why you're not stuffing your face with food that will end up being detrimental to you.

For me, the biggest reason I eat reasonably healthy is because I want to be able to exercise with my son, and more importantly, I want to be as healthy for as long as I can be so I can spend as much time as I can with him.

Don't get me wrong, I'm still partial to a KitKat Chunky, a bag of crisps, a Chinese takeaway and a thousand other naughty but nice food types.

Let's also not forget to mention one of the greatest creations in the history of the Earth i.e. Ben & Jerry's Chocolate Fudge Brownie. It's yummy in my tummy!

All of this is fine, but fine in moderation.

What is moderation you may ask?

There is an incredibly good chance that your body shape will tell you what the definition of moderation and excess is.

However, if you're like my mum and are the type of person that stays slim no matter what you eat; you also need to watch your cholesterol levels.

The late great motivational speaker Zig Ziglar said it best when he said:

"When you're tough on yourself, life is going to be infinitely easier on you."

One of the biggest things that I've learned in life is that the more time I put into something the better I get at it.

If we want to excel at something then we have got to be willing to put the time into it.

Sometimes we won't want to put the effort in, sometimes we just want to chill out and take time off.

There is nothing wrong with taking time off. In fact taking a break is a vital part of success.

The last thing you want to do is get to the stage where you are always tired because you work, work, and work!

But there is a fine line between taking time off so it can be productive for us and taking time off that it leads to never achieving our dreams.

We have to be careful not to let our focus slip, because if our focus on the goal slips we end up creating a new habit that can lead us away from our goals.

If I've done quite well in running, it's not because I was born a gifted runner, it's mainly because I focused on being a good runner, created a habit of running a lot, and put in more hours training than most people do.

So whatever goal you want to achieve then be willing to discipline yourself, be bold, take action and create a habit that will lead you to achieving your goals and your dreams!

So just to recap on the past few chapters:

- **Know what you want.**
- **Visualise what you want.**
- **Focus on what you want.**
- **Take action.**
- **Create a habit that will pull you towards your goal!**

PRIORITIES

Life is a juggling act and you must juggle family, work, and social time altogether. This isn't always easy to do and sometimes you have to make decisions that you feel are the best for you.

The most important thing in my life is to make sure my son has the best life possible and for him to know that he is loved, no matter what he does or doesn't achieve in life.

Of course, I'm very proud of him when he does well at something, but the only thing he needs to do for me to love him is just be himself.

So for me, my time with my Léon is priceless!

Years ago, I was involved with a network marketing company and I listened to a guy by the name of Jerry Scriven, he talked about the importance of time and he said that some people will say one thing and do another.

He talked about an example of a guy drinking down the pub all the time.

The guy down the pub told everyone that his children are his priority.

Jerry pointed out that if he's in the pub all the time then the pub is his priority and not his children.

He then said a quote that has been credited to the philosopher and poet Ralph Waldo Emerson:

"What you do speaks so loudly I cannot hear what you're saying."

That's powerful stuff!

Many times people will say things and then do something completely different but will try to justify themselves and their actions to make themselves feel better.

Sometimes you must take a step back and take a good look at who you are and the actions you're taking.

Many people won't do that, they just drift through life kidding themselves and living a lie.
Many people feel helpless and doubt that they have the ability to change but the good news is that you can change, and you can become the person you dream of becoming!

Some people talk a good game, they 'talk the talk' but they don't 'walk the walk.'

They do little to make their life better and just complain about all the reasons why they haven't done anything significant with their lives.

I'm guessing that you're a little different because you've picked up this book.

You're probably the type of person that wants to make a difference in your life and you're the type of person that is more likely to walk your talk.

There's really no need to bullshit yourself or anyone else!

It only takes a little bit more dedication and work to live a happier more fulfilled life.

Is it worth it?

Well only you can decide that, but from my own experience with putting in the extra effort it has been totally worth it!

Juggling time with my son, writing this book, physical training, interviewing people (when I first started on this book), and putting on public speaking shows for my friend and business partner Mark Billy Billingham (from Channel 4's SAS: Who Dares Wins TV show) and everything else that goes on in my life hasn't always been easy.

Most of the time when it comes to being with my son Léon I've always put my work on the back burner, because for me spending time with him is more precious than any amount of recognition or money I will ever receive.

There is a point that you can get to in life when you realise the material things will never compare to having a connection to somebody very special and wanting to spend as much time as you can with them.

Overall, Léon's mother has been brilliant. Sure we've had our little challenges but that's life and ultimately the best thing to do is to try and make things as good as possible for people.

Before the 2020 Coronavirus lockdown I saw Léon every other weekend, every Tuesday after school and on Wednesday mornings I drop him off to school.

Sometimes we've had to juggle things around especially since 2015, when my life started to change more with interviewing successful people in London.

As I'm writing these words, I've got Léon on a Sunday night instead of having him on Tuesday night because I'm booked to go and interview a top adventurer by the name of Sean Conway, who was the first man to swim the length of Great Britain.

Sean is a hard man to pin down, but I had to take the opportunity to interview him whenever he was available.

There was a point where I almost cancelled it and just let things go on as normal just so Léon could keep to his routine but sometimes you must take these opportunities when they come up.

However, I'm always mindful and careful not to miss too much time with Léon, and if I miss one day with him I'll always ask his mum if I can have another day to make up for the lost day.

The trap many ambitious people fall into is when opportunities come up; they always take them and miss that precious time when their children are growing up.

It's not easy keeping a balance, but you have to decide what's most important to you, is it your career, your status, or your family? Everyone has different views on this and I'm not saying what you should choose either way, but you have to think about how you'll feel in the future about some of the choices you make.

You don't want to look back on your life and think "If only I spent more time with my children or loved ones."

You also don't want to look back on your life and think, "I wish I would have taken that opportunity."

Keeping a balance is an incredibly challenging thing to do, but at the end of the day it's up to you to decide which way to go.

So why is there a chapter in a book about achieving big things talking about priorities with family?

The reason for this is that many books on succeeding focus mainly on money or becoming one of the best in your field - but if you only focus too much on money and status then your life will not have overall success and even more importantly…a healthy state of mind.

Most of us want a rounded success.

Pretty much all of us want happiness, health, successful relationships with loved ones, a certain degree of financial success and a good social standing; so we have to prioritise what is most important to us, and make sure that we are putting the right amount of time and effort into each individual priority.

That way we will live a happier and more fulfilled life!

IF YOU DON'T ASK YOU DON'T GET

"Ask, and it shall be given you; seek, and ye shall find; knock, and it shall be opened unto you."

- Matthew 7:7

One person that is great example for asking for what you want and getting it is Richard Branson.

Branson has spent thousands of hours asking people for help.

Even though now he's in a position where he's the one that helps a lot of people, he still needs lots of help to keep his businesses running, and also, with setting up new projects and making more of his own dreams come true.

Even though some people think he had a lot handed to him on a plate, he has experienced a tremendous amount of rejection.

Rejection is just part of life no matter who you are, God only knows I've been rejected many times for lots of things, but you have to keep going and asking otherwise you lose out.

Although I'm confident that some opportunities will come around again, it's always better to ask.

Sometimes, you will get things without asking but most of the time if you don't ask, you don't get!

People that are high achievers will respect you for pursuing your dreams because they know the challenges you're going through.

They are also more likely to help you because they have been on a similar journey.

When I do something tough I never give much thought about what people will think or say.

If it is something like an endurance challenge, then I am doing it because I want to see what I am capable of, and if I do it for charity it can raise cash for a worthy cause. That's good enough reason for me!

When you're on a path towards a goal and you want to attract things into your life the saying: "seek and ye shall find" is true.

Of course, you won't always find what you want, and you won't always get what you want, but by seeking and taking action you are far more likely to get the results that you want.

I decided to book a nice hotel on a weekend for a former girlfriend and myself and when we arrived we were impressed by the inside of the hotel.

It had undergone a huge refurbishment and the staff were kind and helpful.

The bedroom didn't disappoint either, my girlfriend was amazed by the girth and the length of the king size bed. So yes, size does matter.

We went for a meal and decided to pig out on a dessert, so we both went for the hot chocolate fondue with vanilla ice cream.

Most of the time when I'm at a fancy restaurant, I have to say that the dessert is usually a bit on the small side.

It's probably just as well, because more dessert equals more calories!

When the dessert came on this occasion, not only was it small, but the hot chocolate cake was only just above room temperature!

So, to my girlfriend's amusement or horror (I'm not sure which), I sent it back and asked for it to be warmed.

I had already taken a bite out of it, so not wanting to be a diva and throwing my teddy in the corner, I 'politely' asked the waitress if she could slap it in the microwave for a few seconds and make it warm?

A few minutes later they came out with a new hot chocolate cake, "now that's more like it," I thought.

I didn't care whether it was my old cake reheated or a new one!

All I wanted was the food described on the menu.

There are a lot of people who won't do what I did. In many cases, people will just make do and complain to their friends about the service or the product without giving the creator (in this case a chef) a chance to put things right.

You can't please everyone all the time, but for me personally, I want to hear constructive feedback so I can make things better.

I like what Abraham Lincoln said;

"You can please some of the people some of the time, all of the people some of the time, some of the people all of the time, but you can never please all of the people all of the time."

If you want the good things in life you must ask, and when you ask, ask politely.

There are several little points to this story:

1. Ask for what you want.
2. If you don't get what you want, ask again politely.
3. Try to get things spot on the first time or you could waste your own time and get negative feedback from people.

One thing that came up was a Christmas charity dinner in Swansea with legendary rugby player Sir Gareth Edwards.

Swansea is only a short trip from where I used to live, so I thought this would be an ideal event to meet Sir Gareth and ask him if I could interview him.

I've found that people are much more likely to give you an interview if you meet them in person, and if you're already supporting an event they're a part of, even better!

I had also booked another interview later that same day in Cardiff with Nigel Walker the former Head of BBC Sport, who was also a former Welsh Rugby International and an ex-Team GB athlete, as well as being (at the time of writing) the Director of the English

Institute of Sport (EIS) and thought I would have plenty of time to talk to both Sir Gareth and Nigel.

While I was at Sir Gareth's event I was sitting at my table thinking about leaving and meeting Nigel on time.

If I'm going to meet someone then that means they've scheduled me into their day when they could have been doing something else.

I always think about treating people how I'd like to be treated, so I'm generally very punctual.

As the Gareth Edwards evening went on, we all finished our meals and we were having coffee.

In my mind I was thinking, "Shall I go up to him while he's having his coffee, or shall I wait until he's finished his talk?"

I decided not to disturb him and wait until he finished his talk.

I thought his talk would go on for a short time, but I was wrong!

As brilliant as the talk was I remember sitting at my table thinking "I've got to go and meet Nigel now" and I knew I was pushing the time by waiting as long as I could.

In the end, I had to leave the room while Gareth was still on stage talking.

I got to Nigel's house just in time and the interview with him was brilliant, but I kicked myself for not seizing the opportunity with Gareth when I should have!

I was even more frustrated after because I had met the event organiser Mandy at the very start and complimented her in putting such a great event together.

Mandy was sitting right next to Gareth and all I would have needed to do was to go up to Mandy while they were having coffee with a smile on my face say, "Mandy this event is awesome (Bearing in mind Gareth was sitting right next to her and would have heard me say that!), I would love to stay but I've got to go and interview Nigel Walker (Gareth would know straight away who I was talking about)."

A bit of name-dropping goes a long way because:

1: They know or are familiar with the person.

2: It gives you more credibility.

3: Many people think, hey, if you're interviewing this person on their tips for success, I've achieved a lot; I'll give you my tips!

I guess you could call that a kind of an ego thing, but the truth is almost everyone (including myself) likes people that acknowledge them for who they are and what they've achieved. I was listening to a guy, who claimed that he has no ego at all.
He was basically saying that he was so spiritually advanced that he's dropped his ego altogether.
That was something that made me smile, because the fact that he said those words showed that he still had an ego.

Not to mention he was on a popular TV show, he has sold millions of books and he goes on speaking tours all over the world.

The point is, everyone, yes even highly advanced people like Jesus, Buddha and Gandhi would like people to listen to them, follow them and take what they have to say seriously.

Another point to the story was, seize the moment!

Sometimes you may not think the timing is right, and you may be fearful that you'll look a fool.

However, if that is the only chance you'll get, just go for it and ask. What's the worst that could happen?

It's just like asking a girl or a guy out.

If you don't succeed with that person you can simply move on to someone else...NEXT!

The story doesn't end there.

I kept pursuing my goal of wanting to interview Sir Gareth and eventually (through my friend Darryl Jones) it happened.

We even became quite friendly; having tea at his house several times and Sir Gareth came to one of the talks, which I produced and hosted for Billy.

So, sometimes opportunities can come up again.

There's a fine line between acting too soon by seizing the moment and being patient and waiting for the right time for something to happen.

Ultimately, what is meant to be is meant to be, and all you can do is your absolute best!

Just keep on asking for what you want, be persistent and I can promise you that most of your dreams will come true and you will create an incredible life for yourself, and the people close to you!

KEEP GOING

"Success is stumbling from failure to failure with no loss of
enthusiasm."
- *Winston Churchill*

There will be many things in your way when you're trying to achieve something and sometimes it's just a case of persisting and never giving up that will get you to reach your goal.

One day I was invited to meet the Jordanian Ambassador by Sailing Champion Tracy Edwards.

I didn't have a shirt to wear for the event, so my mate lent me a nice pink one.

It fitted me ok, but the only challenge was it needed ironing.

No big deal I thought, so I got the iron out of the hotel cupboard, turned it on and waited for it to heat up.

Unfortunately, it was broken!

I phoned the reception for another one, but I was extremely pushed for time at this point.

I had no idea how long the hotel would take to deliver the iron so rather than wait for the hotel to bring one up I decided there was a quicker way to get an iron.

I began knocking on doors in the hotel so I could ask someone to lend me the iron in their room.

With the first door there was no answer, with the second door the occupant was in the bath, so that was a no too! I tried the third, fourth, fifth, sixth, seventh, eighth and ninth but there was no reply! I kept going and was starting to run out of rooms to ask on my floor when I saw someone going into his room, so I said, "Hiya mate, sorry to bother you but my iron is bust and I'm in a rush to get somewhere.

Any chance I could quickly borrow yours please?"

He kindly gave me his iron; I quickly ironed my shirt and made it to the event on time.

Of course this is just a little example of taking action, asking, and never giving in but whether it's a small goal or a big goal, persistence makes the difference!

How many people would have asked someone to borrow an iron? Not many!

Most people would have waited around for the hotel to bring up the iron, even if that meant them being late.

Maybe that's just my punctual military training kicking in (always be 5 minutes early for an appointment and all that stuff!), or maybe it's that I think it's polite to be on time when someone has invited you to something?

The point of the story is asking, and persistence works!

I'm yet to come across someone who has succeeded in something big by not being persistent.

Yes, there are people who have been lucky with certain things and have been handed things on a plate, but the high achievers of this world are persistent and keep going until they get the result they want.

Some people are amazed how many incredible people I've interviewed, and I'm often asked how I got these people to agree to do an interview.

The truthful answer is...I asked, and I kept asking.

I know many people think that it can't be that easy, but it simply is.

When I started interviewing people years ago, the world record holder for the high hurdles was Colin Jackson and I really wanted to interview him.

So, the way I went about it was to tweet him using Twitter.

No reply!

About a month or so later I sent another tweet, and again still no reply.

Several months later, I was asked to go to a charity dinner and was subsequently put in the VIP section, and guess who was there?

Yep...Colin Jackson!

Earlier on in the year I had attended a running event that Colin had organised. In the event they handed out T-shirts that said the name of Colin's charity, 'Go Dad Run.' Now what T-shirt do you think I wore to the charity dinner?

Yep, you guessed it! It was the 'Go Dad Run' T-shirt and when Colin saw this he was delighted.

I was introduced to Colin by my friend Cheryl Hicks and asked if he would be up for an interview sometime, to which he said yes. Bingo!

It took months after that to make the interview happen, as Colin's schedule was so busy.

However, eventually we set up a day for the interview and agreed to meet in a coffee shop near the motorway.

I knew a busy coffee shop wouldn't be the best place in the world to interview people because of the noise, and I wasn't sure if they would let me interview him there.

So, before the time of the interview I decided to arrive early and do a little recce of the area.

The only place I could find that would let me do the interview was a gym that was being built.

It was a bit of a mess and it was a little bit like a building site inside, but it was the only option I had where it would be quiet.

I also coincidently met a guy in the coffee shop, who I had recently met at another charity dinner. He said that if the gym didn't come off then I should give him a call and we could use his building for the interview.

An hour or so later Colin arrives, we have a coffee and then I tell him I've got a location to do the interview.

We walked over to the gym and to my horror I found that they had locked it up!

The owners had decided to leave the building, which left me in the lurch, and I was now standing outside with Colin and my cameraman (Kristian Kane), looking at me.

I put on my bravest face, smiled, and said no worries; "I'll get another place now."

In the meantime, Colin was left standing outside with Kristian which was not good!

I thought to myself, no problem, I can phone this guy who offered me the building and Plan 'B' will come into effect.

So, I'm now standing outside ringing this guy in front of Colin and Kristian and guess what, he doesn't answer the phone; Plan 'B' has gone... what we call in the UK, "tits up!"

Now I'm going to have to make up a Plan 'C' on the spot!

I went to one building and asked them if I could use their building to interview Colin, but they told me that they couldn't give that decision without the Manager being there and he wasn't on site.

Time for Plan 'D'...the next few buildings I went to were unoccupied and locked!

Plan 'F' was a wine shop.

I told the guy in charge about the situation and said, "I have Colin Jackson waiting outside and I really need a place to do the interview please?"

I asked him if I could use the Manager's office and he said that it wasn't possible because it was a bit messy in there, but he did tell me there was one place they could let me use.

Brilliant I thought!

I got Colin and Kristian and made our way into the wine shop; because of the way things were going I decided to offer Colin a bottle of wine.

This wasn't a great situation either because I knew I hardly had any money in my bank account at the time, which meant if he picked a very expensive bottle of wine it would've been very embarrassing for me when the cashier tells me my card has been declined.

Colin didn't go overboard, and he picked a £12 bottle of wine, so I was grateful that he didn't go for any Dom Pérignon or Cristal, because if he did, I would've been completely fucked!

I ended up interviewing Colin in the wine shop's store cupboard.

It was a far cry from the BBC studios and the prestigious studios around the world that Colin is used to, but it was better than nothing. To his credit, he never moaned or complained about a thing and did a brilliant interview.

In the end I made the best out of an awkward situation, so the moral of the story is;

Never give up and if you don't ask you don't get!

LUCK

"My success was due to good luck, hard work, and support and advice from friends and mentors. But most importantly, it was dependent on me to keep trying after I have failed."

- *Mark Warner*

Luck is a subject that is talked about a lot in the world of personal development and many people who have achieved things on a high level will say the old cliché, "the harder I work the luckier I get" and will want to take all the credit for succeeding! While there is a lot of truth in that, the full truth is that there is more to succeeding than just putting in hard work.

If you were born in an extremely poor country, with a brutally controlling government and you had severe mental or physical disabilities, I think you'd agree that it's harder to succeed?

The most honest high achievers will tell you that they did put a lot of effort into making their dreams come true, but they will also tell you that there is an element of luck to their success.

Just before I wrote these words, I was watching David Letterman interviewing George Clooney and they both acknowledged that there is a lot of luck involved with their success!

I can't say that I'm a natural writer but becoming an author was a dream come true for me.

When I was 16 such a thought was simply impossible to comprehend! I mean come on, a kid that didn't do well at English in school becoming an author, what are the odds on that?

However, what I will say is that becoming an author was mainly down to putting the hard work in with a combination of luck!

The luck part was mainly because I could now self-publish my books via platforms like Amazon, Apple, Kobo, and many others.

I once heard a quote from a guy by the name of Dexter Yeager, who was a car salesman and later became a huge success in the Amway network marketing business.

Dexter said, "If the dream is big enough, the facts don't matter!"

It's a good quote but there are certain circumstances where no matter how big you dream; your goal will not come true.

For example, you may play the lottery and have a big dream that one day you'll win the biggest ever jackpot.

However, something like that is mainly down to luck.

There may be someone who dreams about winning Wimbledon, but if she or he is a double arm amputee, it's not going to happen!

You may have someone who has a big dream that one day they'll break the 100m sprint world record, but they don't have the fast twitch fibres in their genetics, so it's not going to happen!

However, in a broader sense of the quote, Dexter is still right to an extent.

If the effort you put in matches the dream that you have, then there is a much better chance that you'll make that dream come true!

Even if you never become the best in your chosen field, you'll still be a lot further ahead in life and closer to your dream by putting in lots of effort than you would be if you didn't give it a shot!

Although I wasn't a natural runner and went on to do well with running, there was a lot of luck involved in that too!

Yes, I put in far more hours on the road than most people would, so I'll take the credit for that!

What I can't take the credit for is that I was very lucky not to have serious injuries, which could have stopped my running.

Sure, I've had loads of injuries that have taken time to get over.

Foot injuries, ankle injuries, calf injuries, knee injuries, shin injuries, hamstring injuries, hip injuries, you name it, I've had most of the injuries you can get with running, but they've all healed.

Some people I know are disabled or have injuries so bad that they can never run again, so you bet I've been lucky!

What have you achieved in your own life by putting in hard work?

At the same time you may also know that you had a bit of luck with achieving that goal.

Myself, and my son Léon used to play WWE wrestling on the iPad, it's a game he loves and to be honest at the time I got a little bit addicted to it as well.

We also started to watch some of the wrestling competitions on YouTube and one night I was watching a young WWE fan by the name of Connor 'The Crusher' Michalek, a 7-year old who had cancer; his hero was the WWE wrestler Daniel Bryan, so of course his dream was to meet Daniel.

Thanks to some amazing people Connor was invited to WrestleMania and his dream became a reality.

When Daniel met Connor he said, "Connor was special for one million reasons, his smile, he was so quick witted and nice to everybody. You couldn't help talk to him and instantly fall in love with him."

Daniel Bryan went on to win WrestleMania and guess who he went to see first when he got out of the ring - little Connor.

Daniel leaned over to Connor and hugged him and said to him, "Connor you mean a lot to me, you give me a lot of strength; you've helped me earn this and please keep on fighting."

Connor's dad said Connor was elated!

One day Connor's Dad Steve got the most devastating news any parent could get, there wasn't much time left for his little angel and Connor sadly died in 2014.

There are many things that increase your chances of getting cancer, which include smoking and drinking alcohol.

Of course Connor was too young to do any of these, so he couldn't be blamed for getting cancer.

The truth is any child, or anyone for that matter could get it!

What is the point of this story you may ask?

The point is;

If you made it to adulthood you are already incredibly lucky and always be grateful for what you have got!

JET POWERED DELUSIONS

"Great spirits have always encountered violent opposition from mediocre minds."

-   Albert Einstein

While visiting my (then) girlfriend in Warwickshire one day, I decided that I would look around for things to do in Warwickshire while she was at work.

This is when I came across the jet powered 'Thrust SSC - the fastest car in the world,' which was on display at Coventry Museum of Transport.

Many years before I had sent an email to the man that made this possible – 'Richard Noble, I told Richard about my dreams and goals and he was very encouraging and supportive.

As I've mentioned before, big thinkers are far more likely to encourage you because they are the type of people who know they have made their own dreams come true.

I knew that Coventry had a massive part to play in the field of transport many years ago. What I didn't know was that the man that invented the jet engine was born in Coventry.

It seemed a fitting place for Thrust SSC to rest, as not only was Coventry the hub of the car industry but the jet engines mounted on each side of the car were invented by somebody who also came from the city.

During the time of World War 1 a young boy was at home obsessing about machines and especially the newly invented aeroplane.

This young boy had seen the aeroplanes being built and saw one crash-land near his house!

Despite that, his dream of becoming a pilot was moulded at a very young age and he passionately wanted to join what would become the Royal Air Force (like my good friend Paul Hughes, who is one of the main editors of this book).

It was reported that the young man physically wasn't up to much, as he was a very short person and initially the Royal Air Force didn't want him.

However, the young man persisted, and he eventually achieved his dream of entering service with the Royal Air Force.

He quickly became an incredibly talented pilot and as a natural risk-taker would always push the boundaries of what the aeroplanes he was flying could do!

As much as he loved flying, he believed that planes could be made much better.

He believed that they could be faster and travel further, but he needed to come up with an idea that would revolutionise aviation.

Of course, when some people found out about this, they thought that he had delusions of grandeur.

The young man's name was Frank Whittle!

Whittle knew that the lower the altitude the aeroplane was flying at, the denser the air, which subsequently increased the drag factor.

So, he wanted to come up with a way of making aeroplanes not only fly faster and further, but also higher.

Quite simply, if aeroplanes flew higher it would be far more fuel efficient due to the notably lower drag.

One of the challenges with flying higher was that the higher the aeroplane would go, the less oxygen there would be to run the engine efficiently.

Not only that, propellers needed more air to 'bite into' to move the aeroplane forward. While other inventors were thinking about how they could make propellers better, possibly with different materials, bigger or smaller blades and the shape of the propellers, Whittle believed that the plane needed something completely new.

After working on his new propulsion system Whittle got a breakthrough and was invited to meet one of the top aeronautical scientists of the day, A.A Griffith.

For Whittle's dream to become a reality, he needed the support of Griffith and the British Government.

Whittle showed them a design, which showed an engine with a fan at the front that sucked in air and compressed it in a combustion chamber.

Then fuel was sprayed into the chamber and ignited.

Whittle believed that the burning gases would propel the plane up to speeds up to 596mph.

Unfortunately for Whittle, Griffith told him that it would never work and refused to help fund the project.

This was a major blow for Whittle, as he looked up to Griffith and believed that his design would work.

Griffith was dismissive of Whittle's idea and there is no doubt in my mind that Whittle would've been devastated by such a rejection.

Griffith said that there was no metal in the world that was strong enough that could stand up to the intense heat in the combustion chambers and the engine would melt!

At that point, many people would've turned around and called it a day, but Whittle believed in his invention, he believed in himself and if anything, it made him more determined to produce the engine that he wanted.

Whittle didn't have the backing of the British Government, but he was resourceful and despite that door being shut to him, he made moves to open up other doors and get private funding.

He then spent the next eight years working on his invention.

It took a lot of time, a lot of patience, a lot of determination and a lot of persistence!

In 1937, Whittle was ready for his prototype engine test.

It was a huge day for him but unfortunately it ended up not going to plan and the test failed.

Whittle wanted to be the first person that invented the jet engine but there was competition from other nations, especially Germany.

At the time Adolf Hitler made the jet engine a priority.

The Germans also had a prototype and they installed it into a German fighter plane. On 27 August 1939, the aeroplane took off and was a success, but only to a degree. The flight lasted only six minutes because the metal couldn't withstand the heat of a jet engine.

Only a month later Hitler invaded other countries and triggered World War 2.

Initially, the British Government didn't consider the jet engine enough of a priority, however, now that Hitler had invaded Europe, they knew they needed the best technology available.

Although the British Government wouldn't support Whittle at first, they changed their mind.

Whittle was given the necessary public funds by the Exchequer and was put in charge of a team of the best available engineers.

The next plan of action would be to get metal manufacturers to come up with a metal that would withstand the extreme temperatures of the jet engine.

Although there was no one metal that was strong enough the manufacturers finally developed a mixture of chrome, nickel, steel, and molybdenum.

Many times in life, you either have to join certain components together or join forces with other people to produce the best results.

Not wanting to shy away from testing prototypes, Whittle climbed into a Gloster Pioneer plane on the 11th April 1941 to conduct some ground tests.

A day later the decision was made to put another pilot in the plane to test the jet engine off the tarmac.

The aeroplane flew for 17 minutes before it landed safely back on the ground; this was a massive success, not only for Great Britain but also for every other country in the world!

While I was doing research on who invented the jet engine, there were several people in the comment section saying that Romanian Inventor Henri Coanda invented the jet engine (like they were there when it happened).

Although, yes, I'm British and it would be quite biased of me and quite normal to say it was a fellow countryman that invented the jet engine, I really don't care. I wasn't there, so I don't know 100%.

Who invented what, and when, isn't that important, and it certainly won't change yours, or my life.

However, Sir Frank Whittle's design was and still is the blueprint for the jet engines today!

The lessons we can take away from this great man are:

- Have big dreams.
- Persist.
- Take risks.
- Push your limits.
- Think of new ways of doing something.
- Even when someone you respect rejects your idea; it doesn't mean that you are wrong.
- If you are rejected, still push forward if you believe in your dream.
- Be resourceful.
- When one door closes, another one opens.
- Be willing to invest a lot of time into your dream.
- You will always have competition.
- People that once wouldn't support you could support you at a later date.
- Join forces with others.

EPILOGUE

With finishing off this book, I'd just like to say a few last words to you.

I've spent a good portion of my life striving for dreams that I wanted to make a reality.

Sometimes I've succeeded and sometimes I failed. But for the most part, I have achieved far beyond my wildest dreams.

They may not be wild dreams or big achievements compared to what other people have achieved.

However, when I think back to when I was that 16-year-old boy with little confidence and didn't believe in myself, I know I've come a long way.

The point of saying this is that I know if I can go from where I was to where I am today then I know you can achieve great things in your life!

Many people first thought I was totally off my rocker and they believed I had no chance of achieving what I have now achieved.

When you want to achieve something greater than you've ever achieved or you want to become more than you currently are, you're going to attract critics.

My recommendation to you would be to keep your dream in your mind, get good people to support you, write down your goals, focus on where you want to go, read or listen to positive books or music, put the work in, take the setbacks on the chin, keep moving forward and eventually you'll get there!

"Here's to the crazy ones. The misfits. The rebels. The troublemakers. The round pegs in the square holes. The ones who see things differently. They're not fond of rules. And they have no respect for the status quo. You can quote them, disagree with them, glorify, or vilify them. About the only thing you can't do is ignore them. Because they change things. They push the human race forward. And while some may see them as the crazy ones, we see genius. Because the people who are crazy enough to think they can change the world, are the ones who do."

- Rob Siltanen.

ACKNOWLEDGEMENTS

It's almost impossible to say how many people have helped me along the way with producing this book, and if you're not in the acknowledgements just know that I am very grateful for your support and help!

However, I would like to say a massive THANK YOU to a few people that I can think of, off the top of my head:

Paul 'The Viking' Hughes, Eva Savage, Debbie Richards, Mark 'Billy' Billingham, Julie Colombino – Billingham, Tracy and Kay Morris, Tom Webb, Ambreen Chunara, Mathew and Nafisa Burden, Lucy Duncombe, Cheryl Hicks, Jamie Baulch, Gene Hipgrave, Kauri-Romet Aadamsoo, Matt Dix, David Poole, Simon Eastop, Mark Dawson, Craig Martelle, Michael Anderle, Sat Sanghera, Michael and Emma Byrne, Paul 'Faz' Farrington, James Atkinson and Laura Taylor.

Also, a huge THANKS to 'The Mark Llewhellin Advanced Reader Team' for taking the time to read the manuscript and make suggestions.

Live Your Dreams!

Mark

ALSO BY MARK LLEWHELLIN

THE UNDERDOG – Achieving Your Dreams Against the Odds

ABOUT THE AUTHOR

In 1990, Mark Llewhellin left school without knowing his grades. He had little confidence and was not at all optimistic about his future.

Not knowing what to do with his life Mark followed some of his friends into the Army. He failed his basic 1.5-mile run, was bullied, and was also voted the fattest person in the Troop!

After a year with the Junior Leaders Regiment Royal Artillery, Mark decided he would try and get into 29 Commando Regiment Royal Artillery, which is an elite Army Commando Regiment that at the time proudly held the Military Marathon World Record (i.e. a marathon carrying a 40lbs backpack).

After failing the 29 Commando Selection phase (called 'The Beat Up') twice, first through lack of fitness and secondly through an injury, Mark subsequently passed on his third attempt and completed the 'All Arms Commando Course' on his first attempt.

Mark later went on to achieve the following:

- Break the 100-kilometre Treadmill World Record.
- Place 1st in the Strava Distance Challenge in 2015 competing against over 51,000 runners.
- Place 1st in the Strava Distance Challenge in 2014 competing against over 40,000 runners.
- Run and walk 70-miles without training on his 40th birthday.
- Become a successful Personal Fitness Trainer.
- Complete the Marathon Des Sables (a six-day, 135-mile ultra-marathon in the Sahara Desert).
- Work and live in London's exclusive Park Lane as a Bodyguard.
- Run 1,620-miles in the United States whilst carrying a 35lbs pack.

Mark has interviewed some of the world's top performers and high achievers in various locations, including one of the world's most prestigious memorabilia rooms…the Hard Rock Cafe Vault Room in London.

He has travelled to over 50-countries and has been featured in leading national newspapers and on TV for his running achievements.

Mark has extensively worked in the support and care industry for many years helping individuals with brain injury, autism, epilepsy, dyspraxia and various types of learning difficulties.

He is the Managing Director of Mark 7 Productions, as well as the Producer and Host of 'An Audience with Mark Billy Billingham' speaking events around the UK.

Mark is currently working on more personal development books and lives with his son Léon (when Léon's not at his Mum's) on a beautiful marina in South West Wales.

A Mark 7 Publications Paperback.

First published in Great Britain on August 2020

by Mark 7 Publications

ISBN 978-0-9956501-2-1

136

DISCLAIMER

Although the author and publisher have made every effort to ensure that the information contained in this book was accurate at the time of release, the author and publisher do not assume and hereby disclaim any liability to any party for any loss, damage, or disruption caused by errors or omissions in this book, whether such errors or omissions result from negligence, accident, or any other cause.

IF YOU ENJOYED THIS BOOK

Your help in spreading the word about Mark's books is greatly appreciated and your reviews make a huge difference to help new readers change their lives for the better.

If you found this book useful please leave a review.

MARK LLEWHELLIN BOOKS OUT IN 2020

GET FREE MARK LLEWHELLIN BOOKS, DEALS AND UPDATES

One of the big reasons I love writing and publishing books is because I build great relationships with my readers.

Join my reader club for information on new books and deals plus:

You can pick up FREE copies of:

1. 'The Underdog'

2. 'Delusions of Grandeur'

Simply go to my website at www.markllewhellin.com and sign up for FREE.

Printed in Great Britain
by Amazon

44643258R00084